CORRUPT
BODIES

CORRUPT BODIES

BODIES

DEATH AND DIRTY DEALING
IN A LONDON MORGUE

Peter Everett
and Kris Hollington

ICON

Published in the UK in 2019
by Icon Books Ltd, Omnibus Business Centre,
39–41 North Road, London N7 9DP
email: info@iconbooks.com
www.iconbooks.com

Sold in the UK, Europe and Asia
by Faber & Faber Ltd, Bloomsbury House,
74–77 Great Russell Street,
London WC1B 3DA or their agents

Distributed in the UK, Europe and Asia
by Grantham Book Services,
Trent Road, Grantham NG31 7XQ

Distributed in Australia and New Zealand
by Allen & Unwin Pty Ltd,
PO Box 8500, 83 Alexander Street,
Crows Nest, NSW 2065

Distributed in South Africa
by Jonathan Ball, Office B4, The District,
41 Sir Lowry Road, Woodstock 7925

Distributed in India
by Penguin Books India,
7th Floor, Infinity Tower – C, DLF Cyber City,
Gurgaon 122002, Haryana

HBK ISBN: 978-178578-552-8
Trade PBK ISBN: 978-178578-597-9

Typeset in Dante by Marie Doherty

Printed and bound in Great Britain
by Clays Ltd, Elcograf S.p.A.

To my wife Wendy and son Alistair, who shared
the nightmare and saw it through

Contents

ABOUT THE AUTHOR

Peter Everett is the former mortuary superintendent
of Southwark Mortuary; he has dealt with over
12,000 deaths, 400 of which were cases of murder.
Everett has since become a journalist, working on
ITV's *The Cook Report* to investigate, among other
things, the illegal trade in human body parts. He now
runs a TV production company, and lives with his wife
Wendy in south-east London. This is his first book.

The Appointment in Samarra

(As retold by
W. Somerset Maugham)

'There was a merchant in Bagdad who sent his servant to market to buy provisions and in a little while the servant came back, white and trembling, and said, Master, just now when I was in the marketplace I was jostled by a woman in the crowd and when I turned I saw it was Death. She looked at me and made a threatening gesture, Now, lend me your horse, and I will ride away from this city and avoid my fate. I will go to Samarra and there Death will not find me. The merchant lent him his horse, and the servant mounted it, and he dug his spurs in its flanks and as fast as the horse could gallop he went. Then the merchant went down to the marketplace and he saw me standing in the crowd and he came to me and said, Why did you make a threatening gesture to my servant when you saw him this morning?

That was not a threatening gesture, I said, it was only a start of surprise. I was astonished to see him in Bagdad, for I had an appointment with him tonight in Samarra.'

1

An appointment with death

7 June 1982

I was awoken by the phone's sharp ring. Barely conscious, reaching for the receiver, I knocked my pipe off the bedside table and swore, waking Wendy.

'Yes?' I demanded, rubbing my eyes. The luminous hands of the bedside clock read 5.50am.

It was a coroner's officer. A body had been found in Streatham. A police car was on its way to pick me up.

'Right, thanks,' was all I could manage as I forced myself into a sitting position, regretting my late night curry with Dr Iain West and Detective Inspector (DI) Douglas 'Dougie' Campbell, along with a couple more detectives from the murder squad. Iain, an inveterate chain smoker, had a warm, compassionate nature and a strong sense of *joie de vivre*. He was popular with detectives because he could outdrink every last one of them apart, it seemed, from Dougie. He was also an incredible pathologist. In 1984 Dr West would carry out the post-mortem (PM) of PC Yvonne Fletcher, shot outside the Libyan embassy, proving that the bullet had come from an embassy window.

I was, comparatively, a lightweight and rarely overindulged, but last night I had definitely had one too many. Five minutes later, I opened the front door to my apartment complex and was slapped full in the face by a gust of wind and several sheets of rain, simultaneously extinguishing both my freshly-lit pipe and my hangover. In my right hand was my murder bag (a doctor's bag containing chalk, string, rulers, compass, magnifying glass, camera, sketchbook and latex gloves).

Ever since I'd accepted the post of Southwark Mortuary's Superintendent, my time was no longer my own. If the on-call pathologist needed help at a murder scene, I was expected to attend. Most murders, it seemed, took place between 10pm and 6am, especially during gales, blizzards and storms. I'd only been in the job a few weeks but I'd attended so many murders I was already on first-name terms with most of the murder squad and felt like one of the team.

We'd been in the middle of an insufferable June heatwave, which seemed to have been broken, temporarily at least, by a thunderstorm that had struck sometime in the small hours. The police car dropped me off in a cul-de-sac of terraced houses beside a busy railway intersection. The local woodentops (police constables) had sensibly created a narrow corridor to the scene in an effort to try to prevent contamination. Many police officers and even some detectives were still largely unaware of forensic procedure (or simply didn't believe in it), so this was an unexpected bonus. Holding up my ID card, I grunted hello and stepped through the inner cordon and onto the verge, tracing my way along a narrow path between some unruly brambles.

Emerging beside the railway tracks I was pleased to notice that it had stopped raining and the clouds were already starting to break. Even better, Professor Keith Mant, the head of Guy's Hospital's pathology department, was already there. A tall, distinguished man with a neatly clipped moustache, Professor Mant was always happy to share the secrets of his phenomenal pathology skills. He came from an establishment family but had refused to join his father's legal practice (the first son in seven generations to do so), opting for medicine instead. During the Second World War, as an army brigadier, he worked for the War Crimes Commission, exhuming Holocaust victims and questioning SS officers, publicly exposing the unbelievably cruel 'medical experiments' the Nazis had performed on their doomed prisoners in the concentration camps. He'd also worked in America for a few years as Virginia's chief medical examiner, and still travelled there to give lectures, something he particularly enjoyed because, he claimed, he was allowed to do so while puffing on one of his large cigars. It was while working in Virginia that Professor Mant would meet and provide advice to a struggling wannabe-crime author by the name of Patricia Cornwell. Nearing retirement, Professor Mant was looking forward to spending more time with his orchids as well as fly fishing, but for now, he wasn't quite ready to give up his first love, pathology, despite suffering from back pain that had become excruciating in recent years. For this reason, Professor Mant tended to require more assistance than most pathologists.

'A train guard spotted the body,' he said as we shook hands. 'A group of railway workers checked it out and dialled 999 a couple of hours ago.'

A pair of constables had managed to requisition a huge tarpaulin from a nearby industrial estate, and were busy rigging it to the trees closest to the body so at least the victim was now out of view of any passing trains.

I opened my murder bag, put on my gloves, removed my camera and took a closer look at the body.

It was a little boy.

'About eight years old, I'd estimate,' Professor Mant said.

He was lying on his back, eyes closed. A large quantity of blood had frothed from his mouth and nostrils, breathed out through punctured lungs. He had several stab wounds to his torso. Two concrete blocks, each about half the size of a football, lay close to his head. Both were marked with bloodstains, and had hair stuck to them. One of the boy's shoes was missing and his trouser flies were undone.

I finished taking photos just as DI Jon Canning joined us. He was in his mid-thirties which was young for a DI in those days, the result of his being selected for the Metropolitan Police's new fast-track graduate programme. He was tall, broad, and his light brown hair was always cropped

Author's disclaimer

It is important to ensure that the secrets and histories of some of the individuals encountered through my work (witnesses, police officers engaged in sensitive work and relatives of some victims, particularly children) are not set out in a manner that would enable people to recognise them. The author has, with the exception of names that are in the public domain, protected the identities of these people by changing names and altering some background details. However, the reader should be left in no doubt that every case is real. Those cases which are a matter of public record are reported in their original detail.

remarkably short. A lit cigarette was constantly held between the fingers of his left hand, leaving his right hand free for detective work.

'Alright if we move him?' Professor Mant asked.

DI Canning nodded.

As gently as possible, I took hold of the dead child's left shoulder while DI Canning, also wearing rubber gloves, took his hip. His skin was still warm to the touch. On the count of three, we rolled him slowly on to his side.

Professor Mant, wincing slightly, leaned in for a closer look, examining the head wounds.

'Yes, I'd say the skull's been crushed,' he said. 'You can lower him back down now.'

'Anyone in custody?' I asked.

DI Canning shook his head.

'Anyone reported a missing child?'

'Yes,' he said, looking at a photograph of the boy given to him by the boy's mother for the missing poster. 'It's definitely him.' The photo showed a traditional portrait shot of a happy-go-lucky child unable to control a cheeky grin. 'Matthew Carter. Eight years old. Parents live over there,' DI Canning added, nodding behind us, 'in the terrace behind the sidings. As soon as we're done here, I'm going to pay them a call.'

A cry from a constable alerted us to the fact that the child's missing shoe had been found. It was about 30 metres from the body, lying close to a gap in a fence. On the other side of the fence, on a small patch of waste ground, close to a line of terraced houses, was a BMX bike.

'Looks like he was running away,' Professor Mant said, turning back to examine the stab wounds. They were each about two and a half centimetres across. He leaned in closer and pressed one of them. 'A blade seven- to ten-centimetres long. The frothy blood is the result of blood in the lungs, so judging by the amount, he was breathing for some time after he was stabbed.'

'So the concrete block was dropped on his head to finish him off?' DI Canning asked.

Professor Mant nodded. 'Possibly. We'll be able to give you a more definitive picture after we've done the PM.' He took out a small kit bag from his coat pocket and took a swab from the boy's mouth and cheek. He winced as he tried to stand. 'Peter, could you give me a hand?' I helped him to his feet and after brushing debris from his hands he said: 'No blood or skin under his nails, so either he didn't have a chance, or didn't try to fend off his attacker.'

I quickly sketched the scene, making sure to include the cul-de-sac, the railway line and the route to the lost shoe and bike, adding some measurements. Then, with the help of a constable, we placed Matthew's body in a bag. Once it had been loaded into the Doom Buggy (the funeral director's van), I travelled to the mortuary with Professor Mant in the back of a police car. I lit my pipe and mulled over this terrible crime. DI Canning had a difficult day ahead of him. He was about to deliver the heartbreaking news to Matthew's mother. And then I started to think about my own problems, in particular what was waiting for me once I reached Southwark Mortuary.

My RECENT APPOINTMENT as mortuary superintendent of Southwark just two months earlier, in April 1982, had come as a complete surprise. I was relatively young and inexperienced, having a hospital (non-forensic) background, and Southwark was the UK's busiest forensic mortuary (with about 2,000 bodies arriving each year). I was honoured to be working under the supervision of the Royal Coroner, Dr Gordon Davies. Davies was an extraordinary man who, as well as being the country's top coroner, had been a successful doctor, army officer, lawyer, psychiatrist and inventor. He was an excellent and intuitive coroner who once advised a colleague, in relation to the case of an old lady found gassed in her kitchen: 'If the budgie has been taken out into another room, it's suicide.'

My future looked bright. I was in my early-thirties, on a high salary, had luxury penthouse accommodation five minutes' walk from London Bridge and would receive forensic training from the top echelon of Home Office pathologists. Unfortunately, what I hadn't known when I arrived for my first day of work one sunny spring day was that no one else had wanted the job. Southwark was seen by those in the know (and as I'd come from a hospital background as opposed to forensics, I hadn't known) as a poisoned chalice.

Southwark Mortuary was atmospheric to say the least. The building stood on the site of Marshalsea Prison, made famous by Charles Dickens in *Little Dorrit*. Both Dickens and William Shakespeare had worshipped at St George's Church next door. The mortuary's outer wall had once been part of the prison, and I would later discover, during renovations when builders unearthed a skeleton, that a large section of the mortuary had been built over the prison cemetery.

My first day had been a shock. Entering the post-mortem room I walked into a scene straight from Hogarth's *Pandemonium*. The three metal PM tables each held a body, all in various states of disarray. Two more lay on porter's trolleys. A senior pathologist's first words of welcome to me were: 'Thank God the cavalry has arrived!' This was Professor Hugh Johnson and, although he held the distinction as being one of London's finest pathologists, he was also an ogre who seemed to hail from the Edwardian age and who'd become increasingly bitter ever since he lost the battle to become the Senior Chair of Forensic Medicine at the London Hospital. He flew into a rage at the drop of a hat and, if sufficiently exacerbated, tossed scalpels like throwing knives around the PM room.

Apart from the three metal PM tables at the centre of the room, there was a wall lined with cupboards half-consumed by woodworm, and at the far end were two dirty aluminium sinks filled with bloody implements. A mortuary assistant, cigarette dangling from his lips, was hosing blood from the floor while a nervous trainee pathologist tried to dissect a brain under Professor Johnson's fierce gaze. 'These morons haven't a bloody clue!' Professor Johnson yelled as he turned back to the trainee and, gesticulating at the brain now cradled in the man's shaking hands, demanded, 'What on earth are you waiting for? Put the damn thing in the bucket!'

Beyond the PM room was a passage, fifteen metres long with nine fridges lining one wall. The end fridge, I later learned, had never been used because the door had been put on the wrong way. The foul room (for dealing with decomposed bodies, aka 'stinkers' to us professionals) was next to the door to the Coroner's Court and Jury Room. Juries, overcome by the odour, often had to be evacuated to close-by Tabard Gardens while coroner's officers sprayed the court with air freshener. Finally, the electronic doors to the body-admitting area from the mortuary's courtyard didn't work (and hadn't for six years), and this meant that newly-arrived bodies had to come in via the front, and could be seen from the street.

As I continued my self-guided tour around the mortuary I found the coroner's officers' unit. Coroner's officers were police constables who, on behalf of the coroner, led inquiries into suspicious deaths. They were the main point of contact for the coroner, bereaved relatives, doctors, the police and funeral directors. I stepped into their office and bade them a hearty good morning, only to be met by eight pairs of hostile eyes. They grumbled something back at me, regarding me with contempt before returning to their typewriters.

That morning, as I'd stepped through Southwark's doors, I'd been ebullient. By lunchtime I was exhausted and glad to flee to my office, clutching my head in despair while wondering how on earth I was going to get out of this. My job as mortuary superintendent seemed to include just about every role in the mortuary itself and, apart from the usual requirements such as assisting pathologists with PMs; liaising with Scotland Yard; dealing with body admissions and collections; checking pathology reports; writing reports and organising rotas, I'd already spent a great deal of time mopping up after incompetent technicians as well as trying to clean, tidy away and organise equipment so it could be found again.

The pace was relentless. Quantity rather than quality appeared to be the norm. I was told it was not unusual for one pathologist to conduct more than twenty PMs in one day. I'd just arrived from St Mary's Hospital, where I'd been the Senior Mortuary Scientific Officer and where the average was about four per day. Here, the mortuary staff would dissect the bodies and place organs in a plastic bucket prior to the pathologist's arrival. Unfortunately, they were often in such a hurry that they would miss essential post-mortem signs such as pneumo thorax or haematomas. At St Mary's, PMs had taken up to three hours to complete; the average for Southwark was ten minutes.

As a clear example, a few days later I saw a well-known pathologist pulling up in the car park. I finished off a telephone conversation and proceeded to make the pathologist some coffee. By the time I entered the PM room with a steaming mug, the pathologist had already completed his examination.

The main reason behind this expedient approach was money. Pathologists received a large fee for every case they examined; this was in addition to their salary and private consultation work. Little wonder they all lived in detached houses and drove expensive cars.

BACK TO MY first day at Southwark. It took a few shoves to force open the door to my office. It was a dusty room, bare save for a bookcase full of files, a metal filing cabinet and a desk with an ancient edition of *Gray's Anatomy* propping up one snapped leg. One wall was bare brick, the old Marshalsea Prison. A dirty, draughty window, painted shut, provided me with a view of St George's cemetery.

I slung my briefcase onto the table, which wobbled and creaked. I took out my sandwich and pipe. I'd been surprised to find we were low in stock of just about every chemical fluid and medical appliance going. This would never have happened at St Mary's, and I wondered whether this was one of the differences between hospital and coroners' mortuaries. I lit my pipe and started to go through my predecessor's ring binders, looking to order fresh supplies. According to the files, we should have had plenty of chemicals, tools and appliances in stock, enough in fact for a small army. So where was it all? I decided to have a closer look through all of the files, starting with a pair of binders stuffed to bursting marked 'personnel'.

Thirty minutes later, both pipe and sandwich lay forgotten on my wonky table, that morning's *joie de vivre* as dead as the cadavers lying in the fridges outside. Turning the pages I learned with increasing dismay that not one, not two, but several mortuary personnel had recently been under criminal investigation, and not just at Southwark but at coroners' courts all over London. The first case that caught my eye was that of the mortuary technician charged with cannibalism. He'd been caught with a human liver, and a search of his home revealed a veritable butcher's counter of human organs in his fridge. Another technician had been arrested for

11

plunging a knife repeatedly into a body, for God knows what reason, perhaps inspired by Sherlock Holmes' beating of a dead body to see if it bruises in *A Study in Scarlet*.

In Southwark, theft seemed to be the order of the day. I could see that someone had altered official records, clumsily deleting item lists to try to cover up the losses. I also came across a letter from a funeral director complaining about how bodies had been sent from the mortuary in coffins awash with blood. This had been the responsibility of George, my deputy. A disciplinary hearing carried out by Southwark Council's Department of Environmental Health (our lords and masters) had led to nothing more than a written warning.

Among the many letters of complaint regarding mortuary errors and misdemeanours from irate pathologists was that of a blunder that concerned the incorrect labelling of two bodies. Both bodies had undergone PMs with the wrong medical histories. Another report detailed a complaint from the murder squad, explaining how George had dissected a suspicious death before detectives had arrived. Yet again, the incident was recorded but no action was taken. A few weeks after this, another case of incorrect labelling resulted in two bodies having the wrong PMs followed by yet another case in which two bodies had been mixed up and given to the wrong families. This was the second time this had happened. On the first occasion one of the families ended up cremating the wrong body before the second family reported the mistake; they had opted for an open casket. Despite this, George had only ever received written warnings.

The mortuary – an extremely secure building – had recently been broken into and an expensive watch belonging to one of the bodies had been stolen. This, on the one night that George had 'forgotten' to place any personal effects into the safe. I should point out here that George lived, as I did, in a flat that came with the job, which was situated directly above the mortuary. The council's response to the break-in had been to install a new safe and fit the mortuary with an infrared alarm system.

It was clear to me that at the first signs of trouble, mortuary staff closed ranks and, for the most part, had been able to keep these incidents covered up. At the same time, no one had felt obliged to try to change anything. No wonder I hadn't been offered the chance of the grand tour of the mortuary prior to my appointment. I'd simply had no idea what was going on.

There was a knock at my door.

'Come!' I bellowed, furious now at having been thrown into the lion's den.

A thick-set, red-faced balding man in his mid-twenties entered, regarding me with contempt. He introduced himself as George, my deputy. Behind him was a stick insect of a man who looked on anxiously. This was Eric, one of the mortuary assistants, a young man from Peckham.

'Ah, George,' I said, trying to inject my voice with a tone of friendly no-nonsense supervision. 'I want to talk to you. I understand you've been filling in for the previous superintendent and have the keys and codes for the doors and safe. Hand them over please.'

'No.'

'Excuse me?'

'No. As far as I'm concerned,' he said in a thick East End accent, 'I'm the *real* superintendent. I run things around here.'

I was agog, speechless.

'All *you* have to do,' George continued as Eric stood by, looking increasingly nervous, 'is keep your mouth shut.'

I obliged by remaining dumbfounded.

'As long as you keep quiet, you can bump your salary up by 50 per cent.'

'What on earth are you talking about?' I finally spluttered.

'Fiddles,' George said, coming closer, until he was right by my desk.

'Fiddles?'

'Lots of deaths arrive here without relatives. Sometimes they've got money or jewellery on them. We take 'em, sell the jewellery to someone in Peckham and share out the proceeds later. It's quite safe,' George said, pointing at the files on my desk. 'All we have to do is doctor the books. And it's been going on for a while. We make about five grand a year this way.'

At the time this was a small fortune. George would have been on about £4,000 a year. My annual salary was £10,000.

'We've got the support of the coroner's officers.'

Coroner's officers were serving police officers. I couldn't believe that the police would be in on this and I told George as much, but he rattled off a few names so casually that I couldn't help but believe him.

George also alleged that some coroner's officers were making good money via a number of scams. They would recommend certain funeral directors for a fee. Funeral directors sold flowers back to florists, and charged the next of kin for inside sets (pillows and linings that go into coffins with the body) and then didn't provide them. Employees even stocked their homes with domestic supplies taken from the mortuary.

As per union rules, the deputy, i.e. George, had automatically been given the post of superintendent after my predecessor had left, until a qualified replacement could be found but, thanks to cutbacks, the council hadn't been able afford to hire someone new for several months. This had given George plenty of time to consolidate his position.

Recovering somewhat and by now feeling the anger rising within, I stood up and walked towards George and Eric. I had never seen another man cower before but Eric, I believe, could have been a world champion cowerer as his knees bent and he turned his head away from me; he was visibly shaking. George, however, remained unmoved.

'George,' I said, barely controlling my voice. 'Today I have had the misfortune of learning that this mortuary is in a state worse than in Dickens' times and I would, as my job demands, like to drag it kicking and screaming into the 20th century. If you don't give me those keys and codes I will kick up such a stink that you'll wish you'd never even heard of Southwark Mortuary.'

George regarded me coldly. 'Fair enough,' he said finally, taking out a bunch of keys from his jacket pocket. 'Just don't get in my way and I won't get in yours.'

By the time they'd left I was in a daze. Pulling myself together, I immediately telephoned a senior manager at the council. He was more than a little disconcerted when, instead of a friendly first day report, I let him have both barrels about the state of the mortuary and George and the thefts from the dead. After a long pause he stuttered that there as there was no proof, I should do nothing and tell no one. The files themselves weren't enough. According to the papers contained within them, everything had been 'resolved' and the relevant persons disciplined, even though I could see that this was clearly not the case. Everything I'd seen and heard, including George's 'confession', could easily be contested in court.

I hung up. Doing nothing wasn't an option for me. These criminals were desecrating the dead, cheating their families of treasured heirlooms and making a mockery of funerals. As to what I was going to do exactly, I wasn't certain, but if it was going to take evidence to force my bosses into action, then that was exactly what I was going to get.

EVER SINCE THAT first day, I'd been trying to think of ways to end George's criminal reign, but with so much work of crucial importance needing to be done, weeks had passed and still I'd been unable to take any action. As Professor Mant and I passed through the mortuary gates on our return from the crime scene, I saw that George was already there, cigarette clamped firmly between his narrow lips, along with Eric, who'd yet to say two words to me. They were engaged in an intense discussion with Ted, a coroner's officer: a posh gentleman who pronounced 'house' as 'hice' and 'telephone' as 'tiliphone' but was, I was convinced, as bent as a five-bob note. They vanished into the shadows as soon as they saw me arrive. As we wheeled the body into the mortuary's reception I spotted Professor Johnson, red-faced, looking as though he was on the edge of fury as always. 'Hello, Professor Johnson,' I said, 'are you taking over this case?'

'No Peter,' the prof replied, 'I'm here for a domestic argument that turned into murder and what looks like a shotgun suicide.'

It wasn't even 9am yet. This was turning out to be quite the day.

2

The road to death

I saw my first dead body when I was nine years old. It was 1955 and I was on holiday with my parents in Saltburn-by-the-Sea, a traditional Yorkshire fishing town that sits on the edge of golden sands, between rows of cliffs in a sheltered inlet. I'd spent a profitable day playing on the sands, but now a storm was approaching from the sea. We were about to head back to our hotel when I spotted a small and animated crowd beside some rocks at the water's edge. Curious, I ran over to see and, with everyone so focussed on what was before them, I was able to slip to the front. Before me, just a couple of metres away, was a man's swollen and decomposing body. Despite the decomposition (and the fact that marine life had consumed large chunks of his flesh), I could see he was about the same age as my father. His right arm, separated from his body, bobbed in the water just a few metres further. Seconds later, a woman pulled me away, covering my eyes with one of her hands, muttering something about 'children shouldn't have to see such things.' My mother, having just caught up with me, thanked the woman and started to offer me comfort.

The strange thing was that I didn't need comforting. In fact, I wanted to return to the water's edge and have a closer look. For some reason, my parents didn't resist when I stayed firmly where I was and, although I was a little further away than I would have liked, I was able to watch as a stretcher arrived and local fishermen started to carry the body away. I asked where they were taking him.

'To the mortuary,' my mother replied.

'What's that?'

'A house for the dead,' she said, finally pulling me away towards the Ship Inn. 'And that's enough of that topic,' she added. 'Don't let's talk about it anymore.' As she made promises of chips and ice cream, I looked at the smoke rising from the blast furnaces of the South Bank steelworks, keeping my thoughts to myself.

I WAS ADOPTED. My origins were a mystery to me. My new parents (Mother was a police officer, while Father was an auctioneer's manager) collected me from the children's home when I was a toddler. Great Grandfather was a millionaire, having made his fortune in shipping, and lived in the Great Hall, a giant country home not far from Middlesbrough that required 28 people to run it. My mother and father lived secure in the knowledge that one day it would all be theirs.

My fascination for death only intensified as I grew. Apart from drawing what other people might describe as 'disturbing', or at the very least 'unusual', pictures of dead bodies in various states of decay, by the time I'd reached my teenage years, I'd lost interest in academia and instead devoted important revision time to reading up on the lives of infamous murderers. When my parents took me to hospital to visit a sick relative, I slipped away as soon as I could to find the mortuary. While most children my age might have preferred to skip through fields of poppies in summer, I delighted in days spent playing among gravestones.

My parents grew sufficiently concerned to take me to see an eminent child psychiatrist called Dr Renwick. Grey haired and ancient, she tried to scare me by telling me *exactly* what happened during post-mortems. I listened, open mouthed with delight, utterly fascinated as I thought of cranial saws, screw-powered retractors and organs dropping into their appointed buckets. My parents realised the sessions weren't having the desired effect when I started counting down the days to my next one. Rummaging around dusty second-hand bookshops run by doddery old folk but a cough away from the Grim Reaper themselves, I managed to find books about hangmen, murders and, on one delightful November afternoon, a beautiful illustrated book on human anatomy.

My despairing parents had one last go at curing me of my death obsession by sending me to boarding school. There was no time for death here. In fact there was far too much *life* as far as I was concerned. The day usually started at 6.30am, when I staggered out onto the quadrangle to join my fellows for a five-kilometre cross-country run. The school had a great sporting tradition, and regardless of capability we were forced onto the rugby field in all weathers. When I wasn't trying to run out of the way of boys much bigger than I who, heaven knows why, actually *enjoyed* these activities, I was forced to learn Latin, physics and ancient history. I refused and failed just about every one of my exams. When my last day at this miserable institution finally came, my parents took tea with the house master. Suspicious, I eavesdropped, and the moment I realised they were planning to enrol me for the upper sixth for re-sits, I packed my trunk, collected my tuck box, loaded them in the car and refused to come out.

'So what are you going to do?' my mother demanded, not unreasonably. Given there were zero opportunities for sixteen-year-old boys in the death industry, I had to think of something else, and the only thing that came to mind was acting. This was the only subject I had even vaguely enjoyed while at school and so, during the strained drive home, I made promises about drama schools and a career in theatre.

We arrived home to find that Great Grandfather's heart had given out. Trying desperately to resist the urge to ask my mother if I could see the body, for I could see she was terribly upset, we assembled at the Great Hall to hear the reading of the will. Not one farthing came to my parents. Two years before his death, Great Grandfather had divorced his wife and moved his mistress into the Great Hall. She got everything. The will was, alas, watertight.

So money was suddenly tight. Great Grandfather had been generous enough in life to make financial worries non-existent for his children, grandchildren and great-grandchildren, but all of us were suddenly out in the cold. I needed to earn my keep so, after a quick run through drama school, I started work as a deputy stage manager at the Flora Robson Playhouse in Newcastle upon Tyne. My short tenure there during the run of *Macbeth* was perhaps most memorable for its many mishaps. For example, a flushing loo could be regularly heard during soliloquies, and one day, instead of wind sound effects, the Rolling Stones' '(I Can't Get No) Satisfaction' was blasted into the stalls during the three witches' scene. We also made a reckless decision to use real swords and, when our lead actor was hit on the hand during a duel, he yowled in pain and accidentally tossed his own weapon into the audience. I ran down to check that no one had been hurt and was met by the broad smiles of a party of schoolchildren, who denied ever seeing the now missing item.

For the next few years, I worked as a jobbing actor on the repertory circuit before ending up in London, where there seemed to be plenty of work. Unfortunately, after performing in several productions in minor roles, the work started to dry up just as I turned 30, in the long hot summer of 1976.

I spent my dwindling savings drinking wine at The French House in Dean Street. There were usually quite a few famous faces present, and one regular I'd come to know quite well was the true-crime author Edgar Lustgarten, who also presented two crime television shows, *Scotland Yard* and *The Scales of Justice*. Whether it was his reminiscences of famous murder cases, or the fact that my own craft was drying up, I know not, but I was suddenly overtaken by the urge to work in a mortuary.

'Oh goodness!' Edgar exclaimed when I told him. 'You don't want to do *that*. Mortuaries are dreadful places in which to work – filthy, dark and depressing!'

The following day I set about my quest. I visited fifteen public mortuaries where I was told each time that there were no positions, especially for someone so young. The last mortuary on my list was Southwark, which lay in the shadow of Guy's Hospital. The superintendent was a sepulchral, hairless and aggressive man called Frank who looked like a cross between Dracula and Igor. He was terrifying but at least he took my details.

'If you're that keen, you could try the hospital mortuaries,' he told me as he closed the door, 'they always need people.'

My feet were aching but, as determined as ever, I travelled across town to University College Hospital's mortuary, part of a huge Victorian complex of buildings in Gower Street, a stone's throw from where my idea started in Soho. To get to the mortuary I had to walk through a garage piled high with vegetables, and then, via a small staircase I passed through a door into a large room with a frosted skylight. Two porcelain slabs stood in the centre of the room; next to the head of both was a small table containing medical implements. Beyond the slabs a series of tiered benches reached up to the high ceiling, their symmetry broken by a sign bearing the legend: 'From the dead we learn about the living.'

I froze in complete absorption, forgetting all about my aching feet, as if I'd just arrived at the end of a difficult pilgrimage. I was in a mortuary, at last, and it was everything I'd dreamed it would be, even if there were no bodies on display.

'Good afternoon, young man. May I help you?'

I almost yelled in surprise at the sound of this gruff voice which came from right behind my left ear. I'd been so carried away by finally having found my way into a mortuary that I hadn't noticed that someone else was in the room. Spinning around, I found myself facing a tall, distinguished-looking man in his sixties, with long grey hair swept over his shoulders, peering down at me through gold spectacles perched right on the end of his nose. He introduced himself as Professor Anthony Smith, who held UCH's Chair of Pathology.

Hearing the purpose of my visit, Professor Smith smiled. 'We might have an opening,' he said. 'Just head over the road to the Wellington where the technicians are lunching. They're the ones to talk to.'

Heart racing, I strode to the pub, an old building of dark wood, frosted glass and countless shadowy alcoves.

There were only two customers, both sitting at the bar, both dressed in jacket and jeans, pints of beer before them. I explained I was looking for work in the mortuary and was immediately met with broad smiles. A drink was thrust into my hand and we adjourned to a table where we got properly introduced. The older man, who was tall and was in his late thirties, introduced himself as David, identifying his younger partner as Mark, a chap nearer my own age.

They were friendly and, as I was soon to learn, very popular characters (they were on first name terms with the heads of every department in the hospital). Plus, they weren't just senior mortuary technicians. David was the chairman of the Guild of Mortuary Administration and Technology while Mark was its national secretary. These were two of the most important men in the mortuary service.

THE BODY, STILL covered with a white sheet, was lying on the porcelain slab. David, wearing a green rubber apron over his shirt and tie, was arranging implements and checking a clipboard. A plastic bucket stood by his booted feet.

My dreams of taking curtain calls at the Royal Court had been replaced with the silent reality of University College Hospital's mortuary, and I couldn't have been more excited.

David, intent on his prep, hadn't yet seen me and, having finished, gently drew back the sheet. I gasped in surprise. I'd been expecting to see the body of an old person but, instead, lying on the white slab was the pale body of a beautiful teenage Japanese girl with long black hair.

David looked up, saw me and waved me in. 'The best way to approach this job,' he said quietly, with a reassuring smile, 'is with an analytical mind. The body is a vessel, nothing more, the person who occupied it has long gone.'

I looked again at the body on the slab. Although she was anatomically sound, there was something rather unreal about her, and I realised that David was right; the missing factor was the spark of life. I could feel no presence; the body lay inert and hollow, uninhabited and emotionless. Mark entered the room from another door and wished me good morning. Although Mark was close to my own age, he seemed much older. Bold in voice and action, he moved with a confidence and authority I envied. He was also wearing a green plastic apron, wellington boots and a pair of rubber gloves. Mark threw me an apron and I put it on.

David stood by the girl's head, clipboard in hand, while Mark selected a scalpel. Mark then confidently made a long incision running from a point just below the girl's chin, down to her pubis, before he folded the back the skin and, using a saw, cut the breastbone free of the ribs, lifted it out and stood aside. I leaned over and looked. The exposed interior was a multitude of rich colours: pinks, reds, yellows and browns, all perfectly fitted together. This was a masterpiece. No artist, sculptor, or poet could ever hope to match such beauty.

After exposing the organs, Mark removed them in three separate blocks. First, he removed the lungs, along with the heart, which lay between them. Next, he cut out the liver, followed by the stomach, spleen and kidneys. Last came the intestines, a great mass of swirly pink and brown tubes. Each of the organs was placed in a separate plastic bucket, which sat at the body's feet.

David studied each organ, looking for any abnormalities.

'Nothing obvious to report here so far,' David said, making notes on his clipboard before taking samples that would be sent out for toxicological analysis.

Mark next combed the girl's hair to create a crossways parting, running from ear to ear. An incision was then made

27

following the line of the parting, after which the scalp was peeled back.

'Just like peeling a tangerine,' Mark explained.

He then used a saw to cut carefully around and through the skull, just as I liked to do around the top of my boiled egg in the morning. The smell of hot bone dust, a cross between ozone and chicken, started to fill the air. This completed, Mark carefully removed the skullcap, revealing the brain lying underneath, still snugly contained within its membrane.

Mark cut through the tentorium, the brain's protective membrane, before severing the spinal cord and the optic nerves, and then the girl's mind, once the seat of her consciousness, the holder of all the memories of her life, fell softly back into Mark's cupped hands.

Just then the mortuary door buzzed open and Professor Smith stepped in, already dressed in apron and boots, still putting on his gloves, which were made of much thinner rubber.

'Ah, the new boy,' Professor Smith said cheerfully. 'Congratulations on remaining vertical!' he added before pushing his gold spectacles back up his nose and squinting at the girl's body. He then checked David's clipboard before turning his attention to the buckets.

'Nothing abnormal to report,' David said as the professor picked up the brain.

'Always start with the brain and heart,' he told me as he squinted at the grooves, running his fingers over its contours. 'Nine times out of ten, that's where the cause of a sudden death lies, especially in a young person.'

Professor Smith replaced the brain and then removed the girl's heart from the bucket and laid it carefully on the mortuary table. 'Aha,' he said, just a few seconds later. He beckoned me over.

'See here?' he said pointing among the pink and white tissue. 'That thick wall of muscle? Too thick. Constricts the heart, eventually stops it beating.'

'Check her medical history,' he said to Mark. 'I bet she suffered arrhythmias. Cause of death is hypertrophic cardiomyopathy.'

Once Professor Smith had finished his examination, David reconstituted the body, carefully placing the organs into a bin liner and putting them inside the body cavity before folding the skin back and sewing it neatly together with needle and string. After making the final stitch, he washed the girl down with a sponge, applied make-up and, with Mark's help, dressed her in a white shroud. She looked like she was sleeping.

'The important thing in this job,' David said, 'is to never get involved on an emotional level, while demonstrating the greatest of respect for the bodies in our care.'

Within a few days I was helping my new friends with the dissection and reconstitution of human bodies of all shapes, sizes and ages. I knew, from the moment that a human brain fell back from the skull cavity into my cupped hands, that I had found my calling.

3

A life in death

January 1980

The man, balding, in late middle age, was laid out on the mortuary table just as he'd been found, with his trousers undone, his flaccid penis exposed and his chest covered in blood. I puffed on my pipe and looked at Pat, my trusted assistant, who'd wheeled him in a couple of minutes earlier, accompanied by a blushing police constable who was clearly just out of cadet school. Pat raised his eyebrows as if to say, 'We've got a good one here!' I wasn't sure if he meant the dead man or the police officer. Newly-minted police officers were nearly always allocated the unpopular task of accompanying the dead to the hospital mortuary and observing the PM (in cases that weren't thought to be murder). Many would turn green as a grape before passing out the moment I lifted a scalpel.

'Where was he found?' I asked.

'Praed Street,' the constable replied, flushing once more. I frowned at him through a haze of smoke.

'Where *exactly* on Praed Street?'

'Um ...', he said uncertainly, consulting his notebook. 'Two-hundred-and-twelve. Next to Ladbrokes.'

I went to my filing cabinet and pulled out an address book. Flicking through the handwritten entries, I soon saw what I was after. Two-hundred-and-twelve Praed Street was home to an infamous bordello that catered for a certain kind of client who gained a certain kind of pleasure from a certain kind of suffering.

Next to Soho, 1970s Paddington was the place in London where every sexual peccadillo was catered for. We kept a directory of all the known dominatrices and brothels so that we could factor sexual arousal into the cause of death. A closer look at the man's chest showed the wounds to be superficial, the result of nothing more than some enthusiastic lashing with a leather whip.

Five years on from my time at UCH, I'd managed to gain enough qualifications and experience to become a mortuary manager and had found a post at St Mary's Hospital in Paddington. This was the same mortuary where, 40 years earlier, Sir Bernard Spilsbury, the godfather of modern pathology, had been working when he helped provide the evidence that led to the conviction of Hawley Harvey Crippen for the 1910 murder of his wife, Cora. Crippen's case earned an infamous position in the annals of crime history after the captain of the US-bound liner on which Crippen was fleeing recognised the fugitive and cabled Scotland Yard. Chief

Inspector Walter Dew leapt onto a faster ship and was able to arrest Crippen and his lover as they disembarked. Crippen was hanged by the hairdresser and part-time hangman John Ellis that same year.

Conditions hadn't improved much since Spilsbury's day. The post-mortem room was a Portakabin, which contained three PM tables and was mounted on the roof of the pathology department, while the fridge and chapel were hidden deep in the basement. In one cupboard I'd found a collection of instruments, many of which I didn't recognise. They were probably used by Spilsbury himself and should have been in a museum. As for staff, it was just me, Pat and the occasional part-time assistant. Pathologists would sweep in like cloak-wearing vampires, bending over corpses and studying them at great length before sweeping out again and on to their next 'victim'.

'I'm betting that the excitement got too much for this poor fellow,' I said as the police officer turned a deeper shade of crimson than I thought humanly possible.

'The casualty sister said it was a h-h-heart attack,' he stammered.

I nodded as Pat passed me the hospital papers. 'Well, in cases like these,' I said, flicking through the sheets, 'one has to be sure, doesn't one? This your first PM?'

The constable nodded.

'Don't worry,' I said, trying to sound as friendly as possible. 'It's really not that bad. The trick is to see the body as an empty vessel— Oh damn, catch him, Pat!'

Between us we deposited the fallen constable onto the adjacent slab. Pat placed a card that said 'Not Dead' on his chest and fetched some sandwiches from a nearby cupboard before putting the kettle on. I put down my pipe and began my prep. 'Mr Whiplash would probably enjoy his PM if he were alive to experience it,' I said as Pat took a big bite of his sausage sandwich.

THE FIRST MURDER of my career (number one of 400) arrived at 6am one Sunday morning. A woman in her twenties without, it seemed, a mark on her. When we undressed her however, I spotted a tiny stab wound above her abdomen.

A grim-faced detective had accompanied the body from the scene, a bedsit in Kilburn. 'Such a waste,' he said. 'She refused to give her boyfriend money to buy drugs and so he stabbed her.'

The PM was straightforward enough; the blade had severed the young lady's aorta, and she had died from internal bleeding in less than a minute. No one came to claim her body, however, and so the state took over. A few weeks later, I was enjoying a late-night coffee in casualty, chatting to the nurses, when the desk phone rang. Everyone else happened to be busy at that moment, so I answered it.

'I'm looking for my sister,' the voice said. 'I haven't seen her for a while and thought I'd check the hospitals.'

'Ok,' I said, fumbling for paper and pen. 'What's her name?'

She told me and I froze. I was talking to the murdered woman's sister. I couldn't bring myself to give her the bad news, a moment she would probably remember with horror for the rest of her life, and hurriedly passed her on to the casualty sister.

As well as examining admitted bodies, I also interviewed relatives about their loved ones' medical histories, to establish whether a pathologist needed to be called. Dealing with the relatives of the deceased was something I found extremely difficult. With the dead you can relax; they're not going to break down and weep at the unfairness of it all or beg you to tell them it isn't true. Relatives do this and much more, and I found it almost impossible to stammer out the necessary words of comfort when the occasion required it.

Entering the relatives' waiting room in casualty one day, looking for the family of an old lady who'd died about twenty minutes earlier, I found two young women in a distressed state: her daughters. I nodded sympathetically as they comforted one another and then, clipboard in hand, asked whether they wanted Mum cremated or buried? They erupted into screams and tears. No one had yet told them Mum had died! Mortified, I made hopeless attempts to apologise and calm them down. From that day forth, I always checked that everyone was up to speed before I took out my clipboard and asked my PM questions.

Speaking to relatives never got any easier. I arrived in the mortuary one evening to find a teenage girl lying on the PM table. She was wearing a brand new party dress, her delicate hands still clutching a present she'd been taking to her first grown-up party. She looked more alive than anyone I've ever seen on that porcelain slab. It was quite some time before I could bring myself to walk to the relatives' room to interview her parents. Nothing I could do or say could make that moment any better for them. They were dazed, shocked beyond comprehension, as I tried to ask them about their daughter's health and medical history. The PM was performed in silence, always the case with children, until the pathologist found the tiny heart defect that had killed her.

A few weeks later I was working on a quiet Christmas Eve when the festive mood was shattered by the arrival of the body of a young man who'd died of a brain haemorrhage. His weeping widow asked me: 'What am I going to tell his daughters? They're sitting by the Christmas tree, waiting for Santa.' Other unanswerable questions were asked by parents who lost their children to cot death or to a violent husband.

Suicides were often difficult to deal with. Spending so much time with their cadavers, my mind sometimes drifted morbidly towards thoughts of the circumstances which had driven these individuals to that point. One morning we received the body of a young man who'd hung himself in a park. His neck was 30 centimetres long, meaning he'd been hanging there all night. The policeman who came in with the body, a beat officer of more than twenty years' experience, said he'd never seen anything like it. The tree from which he'd been suspended was next to a busy road. 'Every set of car headlights lit him up,' the constable said, shaking his head, 'and yet no one did anything.'

We regularly saw bodies that had been hung. One memorable case, which occurred in 1982, was that of Clare Andrea 'Andy' Neilson, 38, who was found in his bedsit. Andy turned out to be the son of Ruth Ellis, a model and nightclub hostess who had the unfortunate distinction of being the last woman to be hanged in the UK, after she shot dead her abusive lover, racing driver David Blakely, in a Hampstead pub. Blakely had previously punched Ellis in the stomach while she was pregnant with his child, causing her to miscarry. Andy was just ten years old when his mother was hanged for murder. He was by this time living with his maternal grandparents. His grandfather, an alcoholic, hung himself in 1958 while his grandmother was left in a near-vegetative state after succumbing to fumes from a gas leak at her home in 1969.

The night after we'd dealt with Andy's admission, I was working late when the phone rang. The caller identified himself as the secretary to Christmas Humphreys, a famous prosecuting QC who'd been involved in several high-profile murder cases that ended in the execution of the accused. In one case – that of Timothy Evans – the executed man was later proved to be innocent (serial killer John Christie had framed him for the murder of one of his victims). Humphreys had, since leaving the law, become a Buddhist. The secretary explained how Mr Humphreys had been the lead prosecutor in the Ellis case and wanted to pay for Andy's funeral. He also told me that the trial judge Sir Cecil Havers had previously paid a yearly sum into a fund for Andrew's education. Clearly, guilt at the unjustness of Ellis' death and its consequences weighed heavily on them both.

It wasn't all doom and gloom. The closer you are to death, the bigger the laughs when the funny moments do come.

Now having passed all my exams (my schoolmasters would never have believed it), I was asked to give talks to nurses and police officers about the mortuary and PM process. During one such talk, as I described how a body was sewn up after autopsy, a fresh example on the table beside me, a nurse enquired: 'How long do the stitches take to heal?' In another demonstration, this time in how to undress a dead body with dignity, I attempted to remove a dead man's boot only to end up flying across the room clutching a false leg.

On another occasion, I was undressing the body of a man with the help of a young police officer. This was one of her first deaths. The man had made the once-in-a-lifetime mistake of turning into Edgware Road from Praed Street on his moped, dramatically cutting the corner at the same time as the No.7 bus was coming the other way and had died of a broken neck. When we removed his trousers, however, we were greatly surprised. He was wearing frilly pink knickers. Once we started laughing, we couldn't stop. It wasn't meant callously at all, of course; there had simply been tension in the air and the shock of the frilly knickers had made a mockery of our sombre professionalism.

I also began to get used to the idea that the famous and infamous all die the same as the rest of us, and I ended up dealing with quite a few 'celebrities' during my time at St Mary's. I was in my Marylebone flat one evening and had just lit my pipe while gazing over Regent's Park in the early evening light. A flock of geese was flying low over the trees and, as I followed them with my eyes, I noticed an unusual amount of blue flashing lights close to St Mary's. Realising something serious was afoot, I decided to see for myself what was going on and walked the short distance to the hospital.

The media had the building under siege with TV crews, reporters and flashing cameras. Sister casualty looked relieved to see me. Smiling, she winked as she told me to head straight for the crash room, adding with a slight smile: 'Don't mention the war!' Having no idea what she meant and with no time to waste, I obeyed her instruction and found half a dozen detectives gathered around the body of a smartly dressed old man. This rather ordinary-looking gentleman with a sneer of pain frozen on his deceased face turned out to be none other than Albert Speer, architect and minister of munitions to the Third Reich, and Adolf Hitler's confidant. He'd served his twenty-year sentence in Spandau Prison and had come to London to record an interview for the BBC. I left the room to find Pat to help assist me with preparing the body for the PM, which I just knew all the pathologists would be fighting over. They liked nothing more than to add a famous or infamous name to their CV. As soon as I entered casualty I was accosted by a grubby little man in a raincoat. 'I'm from the News, mate,' he said, speaking out of the corner of his mouth. 'Ten grand in it for you if you can snap a photo of the Nazi.' He opened his coat, revealing a pocket camera. I declined and escorted the man to the door where police officers placed him back behind their now more firmly established cordon.

A full investigation had to be carried out but the cause was simple enough: heart attack. The following morning, I escorted Speer's daughter to view his body in the Chapel of Rest. I could tell she was trying to hold it together by being fiercely cold, even commanding me '*Schnell!*' ('quickly!') as the chapel could only be reached by traversing a number of long underground corridors which seemed to go on forever. Once there, she stayed a few seconds and bowed her head before walking quickly out, her face wet with tears.

The next infamous body to grace St Mary's mortuary arrived in the cab he'd just died in. This was Baron Bradwell, better known as Tom Driberg, the communist MP for Barking, who'd once counted the Kray twins, the infamous East End gangsters, as friends. Driberg was also rumoured to be a spy for the KGB, but no one ever seemed able to offer any proof of this. Thanks to the fact he was such a famous public figure, a detailed PM and investigation had to take place but, like Speer, Driberg had simply died from a heart attack.

The Cold War provided me with a few tricky situations. Woken from a deep sleep one night before dawn by the casualty sister in a flap, I arrived at the hospital to find a panicked young constable guarding the dead body of a man in his early forties. Resting on his chin were the remains of a pink tablet that had, presumably, fallen from his mouth. I was soon interrupted by the arrival of a mysterious man who introduced himself as the dead man's 'associate'. He was followed by half a dozen Special Branch officers, one of whom let slip that the dead man had been a KGB officer. They loaded him into a blue van and vanished, leaving me with paperwork but no body or mortuary report for the Coroner. Four hours later, the day casualty sister informed me that she had a dead diplomat in the crash room. I explained that the diplomat's body had already been removed hours earlier. 'Then can you tell me whose body is currently lying on my crash trolley?' I rushed up to find a second man, also with a pink tablet, this time in his mouth. It wasn't Aspirin, and our medics couldn't identify it. Special Branch returned and loaded the second diplomat into the blue van, leaving me with two admission forms but no bodies and a lot of explaining to do.

I also had another brief meeting with Special Branch after a young Irishman had been brought to the mortuary. He'd choked to death while eating a steak dinner. There didn't seem to be anything suspicious about it but, after Special Branch turned up, I learned that he was in fact an IRA sleeper, who, having received his coded message to set off a bomb, decided to have his lunch first – a decision which saved many lives.

LIFE AS A mortuary manager was never dull, and I certainly didn't regret my decision to switch from acting, even when I was called into casualty to collect a dead body and saw it was my old friend Edgar Lustgarten. This was the man whose work had re-inspired me to think about a career in the mortuary. Seeing Edgar made me reflect on my career so far, and I decided that, although I'd loved the six years I'd spent St Mary's, I wanted to do more. The next step up would be to run a forensic mortuary, where larger and headline-making criminal cases were dealt with alongside more complex, unexplained deaths. A few weeks later I was reading the evening newspaper when I saw a position at Southwark was available.

'That would be stimulating,' I thought to myself, filling out my application, never thinking for a moment I'd actually get the job. If I'd known what I was letting myself in for, however, I would have ripped up the form and stayed firmly where I was.

4

Murder most senseless

7 June 1982

Once we'd unloaded Matthew's eight-year-old body onto a trolley and wheeled him into the reception room, I was met by the police photographer and one of DI Canning's detectives responsible for identification and exhibits, followed by lab liaison officer Clifford Smith. Cliff, formerly of the Royal Military Police, was a thoughtful and unflappable character who I would come to know well over the coming months.

We lowered the child's body from the trolley, still enclosed in the bag, onto a plastic sheet on the floor. The photographer took pictures of the body still in the bag, then with the bag open, then out of the bag and lying on the plastic sheet, and then, after carefully undressing him, the body was photographed once more and then placed back on the trolley. The sheet it had been lying on was photographed and then placed into the body bag which was then sealed in an evidence bag, as were the clothes, each item sealed and labelled by the detectives, with me as witness. Matthew's body was then taken through past the fridge room where it would normally stay until it was time for the PM but, since this was an urgent case, and the mortuary was now open for business, we would do the PM immediately.

As we entered the PM room, which was in darkness save for one overhead lamp, I spotted the shapes of three odd-sized figures waiting for me. With the light behind them they looked like three peculiar coffins stood on their ends. I sighed. My staff was a motley bunch, to say the least.

There was Frank, a coroner's officer, who hated to leave his desk, whatever the reason. Trying to prise him from his chair was like trying to raise the dead, so I was surprised to see him up and about so early this morning. Frank had the dressing skills of a five year old, in that his tie was never tied properly, one or other of his shoelaces was usually undone, and his shirt was always untucked. Appearances were deceptive, however. As a coroner's officer (all of whom are serving police officers), Frank was the next most important person after the pathologist. His job was to collate all the police reports on a death (such as reports from the scene, the police laboratory, witness statements and so on) along with information garnered from the PM, and to create a document for the coroner, in this case Gordon Davies, so he could decide whether or not to hold an inquest, and who should be called to appear. We rarely saw Davies, who, along with his deputy, the wonderfully-named Sir Montague Levine, liked to steer clear of the mortuary if at all possible. Knighted for serving as Harold Wilson's personal GP while Mr Wilson was prime minister, Sir Monty proudly sported a handlebar moustache and was a true gentleman of the old, old school.

Towering over Frank was 'Lurch,' one of the porters/ cleaners. A six-foot-six Brummie, he had a curious lurching side-to-side walk. Let's just say that as far as appearances went, it would have surprised no one to know that Lurch worked in a mortuary. He was a terrible cleaner, however, and I spent a great deal of time mopping up after him. He seemed to think that cleaning meant smearing every available surface with an excess of bleaches, powders and creams. Both Frank and Lurch were smoking, but this wasn't unusual. Everybody smoked in the mortuary; it was encouraged. The lighting of cigarettes – or in my case a pipe – provided us with a few minutes of informal debriefing time before or after a PM. If we were waiting for a murder victim to arrive, everybody would be tense and so would light up. By the time the PM began, especially with the mortuary's poor lighting, it was like working in a fog. I was relieved to see that the third man present was Tom, an ex-soldier from the Royal Tank Regiment turned mortuary technician. He was a tough, quiet man, a hard worker.

The three men were chatting away but stopped as soon as we entered. As soon as Frank saw us wheel in the boy's body, he dropped his cigarette into an overflowing ashtray (which Lurch showed no signs of being in any hurry to empty) and scarpered back to the safety of his desk. Only about half of the eight coroner's officers at Southwark ever joined us during a PM. The other half preferred to wait until everything was over and collect the technician's report, along with the pathologist's notes, directly from my office.

Professor Mant arrived moments later and we quickly got to work. We took hair and urine samples, double-checked under Matthew's fingernails for debris, taking and bagging some scrapings using matchsticks. His body was then carefully examined for external injuries and, under Professor Mant's direction, I recorded the location of bruises, cuts and abrasions on a body map.

The body, just over four feet tall, was well-nourished but was extremely pale thanks to the loss of blood. His injuries were extensive. It looked as though he might have been assaulted before being stabbed and before having the concrete block dropped on his head.

'There are signs of compression to the neck,' Professor Mant said. 'Petechial haemorrhages in the upper and lower eyelids.'

This was a sign of blood vessels bursting due to strangulation.

'And there are several abrasions to the neck itself and bruising, as well as two semi-lunar abrasions on the right side.'

The lunar abrasions suggested a stranglehold.

We then counted thirteen stab wounds on the upper left chest, in an area just thirteen centimetres square. Three more stab wounds sat just below this cluster while a further four were in a horizontal line across the upper abdomen. Five of the stab wounds had entered the heart with another one having punctured the liver. The internal organs were all pale while the left lung contained a lot of blood. The head was covered in bruising and abrasions.

'The skull is broken in numerous places,' Professor Mant said, 'with the scalp having become – in places – entirely separated from the underlying tissues.'

As soon as I lifted out the brain, I could see it had been badly damaged.

'The midbrain is crushed,' Professor Mant said, 'while the posterior has been severely lacerated.'

'So this is consistent with a heavy object being dropped upon it?' DI Canning asked.

'In my opinion, most certainly,' Professor Mant replied.

'Such as the blocks of concrete we found at the scene?'

'Yes.'

'And the stab wounds?'

'A single-edge thin-bladed knife about seven centimetres long – assuming its full length entered the body – and one centimetre wide.'

'Any clue as to the order of the injuries?'

'No. All I can say is that thanks to the amount of blood in the lungs, the boy was still alive when he was stabbed and still breathing when the concrete blocks were dropped on his head.'

We were interrupted at this point as a detective had arrived to let DI Canning know that the boy's mother had arrived to make the formal identification. In cases of murder and suicide, all bodies had to be identified by the next of kin.

DI Canning thanked Professor Mant, who left to type up his official report, while Tom and I reconstituted Matthew's body. Each organ was placed in a plastic bag and lowered into the body cavity. As we went about our work, neatly stitching the Y-incision closed, it was hard not to imagine the ordeal Matthew had suffered, how hard he had tried to live, how long he'd tried to hang on, and all this time his killer had remained fuelled by the abhorrent desire to extinguish this young life.

Even Tom, a man of few words, and a man who knew better than most how unspeakably cruel humans could be, was moved to ask the inevitable question: 'What kind of a person does such a thing?' I just shook my head in reply and did my best to cover Matthew so that his injuries did not show their full extent.

Once we were done, Lurch wheeled the boy's body the short distance to the viewing room, which sat between the court and the mortuary. It was a tiny, cramped space, nothing more than a small corridor with a glass window to separate the body from the viewer. The body could not be touched because of the possibility of cross-contamination. I was still tidying up when I heard the mother's awful, indescribable wail of grief.

I decided that this would be a good time to deliver some paperwork directly to the coroner's office and made my way through the building's narrow corridors to the rooms where the eight deskbound police officers were housed.

I'd only been in the job a couple of months but had come to know the coroner's officers quite well. There was

David, who could not bear anything to do with death and 'secretly' nipped whiskey from a flask all day long (everyone knew and pretended that they didn't), but this was hard to hide when he started trying to say hello to the coat stand; Stephen, a red-headed Yorkshireman who claimed to have a 'good sense of humour' and who enjoyed nothing more than playing practical jokes on people, from whoopee cushions to exploding cigars; Ted, a wire-haired man in his fifties who spoke like Prince Philip and behaved like he was a super-intendent instead of a lowly constable (he rarely deemed to speak to anyone in the mortuary); Martin, an elderly man of narrow and short stature who inspired nothing but suspicion; and Paul, a switched-on officer who regarded everyone with suspicion. I got on with two of the officers: Brian, a happy-go-lucky young man with a young fam-ily and Norman, a canny officer close to retirement who chain-smoked and seemed to know about everything that was going on. Although he had a heart of gold, he was just hanging on for a couple more years until he could claim his lucrative police pension. I knocked on Norman's door and held out Matthew's file.

'Alright, Peter?' he enquired, taking the file. 'That deputy of yours still a pain in the arse?'

Norman and Brian were the only two officers I felt I could speak freely with because both of them had warned me about George from day one.

'He most certainly is.'

He flicked open the file and sucked in his breath. 'Nasty case this.'

I just had time to outline the story before I was cut off.

'Everett!' The booming voice of Professor Johnson ricocheted down the narrow corridor. He was leaning out of the PM room, his red face on the edge of fury, as usual. 'There you are!' he exclaimed. 'We're a man short and I need you to assist. Come on! I haven't got all day!'

The PM was of a 55-year-old man who had two knives sticking out from the centre of his chest. Trying to keep the obvious cause-of-death gag to myself, I asked what we knew so far. Tom was present, along with a detective I hadn't seen before who introduced himself as DI Jack Brown, a middle-aged beer-bellied man of good humour; one of those people who'd been there, done that, seen-it-all and written the textbook.

'It was his silver wedding anniversary,' DI Brown said, 'and according to neighbours the happy couple spent the day drinking and arguing. This went on until this morning when Mr Waters here woke up, got a knife and stabbed his wife in the chest.'

I looked around for a second body.

'No, she's fine, relatively speaking,' DI Brown said. 'Mrs Waters picked up two other knives and stabbed Mr Waters with both of them.'

She had obviously done a much better job than her husband but, according to DI Brown, she now desperately regretted her actions, having told the detective that Mr Waters was 'all I got', and that she loved him from the bottom of her heart.

I DIDN'T HAVE to wait long to learn who had killed Matthew. He had left home at 5pm on the evening of his murder to meet an older friend, a fifteen-year-old boy who lived nearby. When DI Canning went to interview the boy, he noticed tiny specs of blood on his trainers and blood and dirt under his fingernails. Before long the teenager was charged with this horrific murder. This case understandably achieved quite a bit of notoriety and was even dragged into the video nasties debate that was raging at the time.

Videocassette recorders had arrived in the UK in 1979, and by 1982 a quarter of UK homes possessed one. Hollywood reacted to this phenomenon by withholding their biggest films from video release, fearing video piracy, which was exactly what this move fuelled. The video market was unregulated, and once businesses saw that people were happy to buy cheap video imports, tiny distribution companies bought up Italian horror movies and US slashers and started shipping them all over the world. In March 1982, distributor Go Video sent a copy of *Cannibal Holocaust*, along with a made-up letter of outrage to self-appointed moral crusader Mary Whitehouse. Mrs Whitehouse, the head of the National Viewers' and Listeners' Association, quickly set about creating – with the help of an obliging media – a full-scale moral panic. Matthew's killer – whom, it was revealed, loved horror literature of all kinds, but especially anything to do with *Dracula* – was used as an example to illustrate the poisonous influence of horror as entertainment, a sign that our society was on the verge of collapse. As a result we ended up with the Video Recordings Act (VRA) in 1983 which banned certain examples of exploitation and horror cinema, i.e. 'video nas-ties'. This act also had the effect of finally dampening the hysteria of newspapers such as the *Daily Mail*, which, in July 1983, launched a campaign with the front-page headline 'Ban video sadism now', describing the 'rape of our children's minds'; in another story the paper suggested that Matthew's killer had been possessed by one such film – when there was no evidence that this was the case.

Indeed, as much as we would have liked to have under-stood why this teen had decided to kill a helpless, innocent eight-year-old boy in such a savage manner, there was simply no answer. He had denied murder and faced trial at the Old Bailey in 1983, where he was found guilty and ordered to be detained indefinitely at Her Majesty's pleasure. Matthew's mother was in court to hear the verdict. After describing the horror of seeing evidence photographs of the block that had been dropped on her son's head, she told the press: 'A day doesn't go by when I don't cry for him. [Matthew's killer's] mother has still got him. All I've got is a tombstone.'

5

The corrupt body

July 1982

The funeral director looked like he was about to start crying. His mouth was open and his lips trembled as if he wanted to speak but didn't know what to say. He was in the mortuary's secure reception garage looking into the back of his brand new hearse.

'What's wrong?' I asked.

'My metal stretcher,' he said, almost in a wail. 'It's gone!'

I looked in the back of the hearse to see that there was indeed, no such stretcher. 'It couldn't be inside the mortuary, could it?' I asked.

We went in and had a look around but there was no sign.

'It was brand new!' he cried. 'Cost me two grand!'

He'd driven down from Yorkshire in his brand new hearse to collect the body of a client. He'd decided to leave his vehicle in the mortuary garage while having lunch, before loading the body and driving home.

Boiling with rage internally, for I knew this was George's handiwork, I maintained a calm exterior and assured the funeral director that I would look into it and would also assist in any way I could with his insurance claim.

George was nowhere to be found, which in my opinion signified that he was at that moment most likely pocketing £500 or so from a bent funeral director, no doubt telling them that the stretcher had fallen off the back of a hearse.

This embarrassing incident was just the latest in a string of impossible thefts from the mortuary which made a mockery of our state-of-the-art alarm system, installed at great expense by the council. One evening, George 'forgot' to put a Rolex watch in the safe and, sure enough, the next morning it was gone.

Few people complained about the thefts from bodies, least of all relatives who rarely knew how much money the dead person had on them, or what jewellery they were wearing. The thieves always left a couple of pounds in the purse or wallet to allay suspicion. On those exceedingly rare occasions when people had complained, nothing could ever be proven. All I knew was that George had let slip that a Peckham-based jeweller bought the jewellery.

More than anything, I was shocked by how blasé George was about it all. The reason for this, I found out, thanks to the minutes of his many disciplinary hearings, was that the union, along with his council bosses, were both on his side. George was adept at spinning a tale about how he was constantly oppressed by his boss (i.e. me), and how the world in general was against him and how he simply had too much responsibility (knowing the council would feel guilty at this, unable as it was to afford to hire any more staff). After one such disciplinary hearing, the miscreant emerged smiling, telling me how he'd been released without charge. The bosses had even told him: 'Don't let the bastards grind you down!'

George was confident in his – as he saw it – unassailable position, with good reason. After having given him so much support over the years, our council bosses would rather save face than find him guilty of any crime; to take any other position would simply be too embarrassing, and might even incriminate them. It was perhaps for this reason that George delighted in telling me about the nefarious goings on in my morgue. For example, he told me how some visiting pathologists were biased when it came to murder PMs.

'How on earth can a pathologist be biased?' I demanded.

'Well, when there's a choice between murder and manslaughter, there's one pathologist who always asks the cops if anyone's in custody. If there is, he'll ask them if the suspect's black or white. If the answer's black, he'll decide the case is murder.'

He also explained how coroner's officers made money by selling transport jobs to undertakers. When an officer needed a body transported to the mortuary he got to choose which funeral director carried out the removal. This duty attracted a large fee, payable by the coroner from the public purse, so those funeral directors who were prepared to share this fee with the coroner's officer got the job. On top of this, when the coroner's officer interviewed the next of kin, he would talk them into using the funeral director who had carried out the removal; as a reward, the officer kept the removal fee and the funeral director got the service fee, and everyone was happy. This simple arrangement had allegedly been going on for years.

George even accused my masters of taking commission from the thefts that he made, which I suspected was another reason why he'd never been suspended.* To hear about such heinous crimes made my blood boil. Although I was the first to tell people that the cadaver is just a shell, the thought of bodies – helpless to defend themselves – being desecrated in such a manner brought tears of outrage to my eyes. Relatives were being denied what would have been treasured heir-looms. It was in this frame of mind that I laid my plans to put an end to the corruption once and for all.

I had a friend who worked for the security services and, after asking him for advice, he gave me the number of someone who supplied private companies with covert equipment which was used to catch thieving employees. A few days later I arrived for work two hours early. After making sure the building was empty, I installed covert micro-phones in several key locations. Soon, I hoped, I would have my evidence.

I stifled a yawn. I'd been late to bed and my baby son had spent the night waking me up at twenty-minute intervals before I'd risen at 5am. Any chance of a quick rest before the

* These accusations turned out to be false.

working day got underway was blown apart when Professor Mant called. 'Good, you're already there,' he said. 'I've got a particularly grim case I need your assistance with.'

Fifteen minutes later, I arrived at a Bermondsey bedsit and was almost flattened by a constable running out of the door and vomiting into a nearby bush. I raised my eyebrows and shrugged in sympathy as I turned and started to climb the stairs. I'd seen every kind of death there was, from bodies swollen with maggots to those with limbs amputated by tube trains, and nothing could shock me anymore.

I yawned again as I entered the bedsit, a huge, gaping yawn that perfectly encapsulated my fatigue. I was still in mid-yawn when I found Professor Mant in the bathroom. My yawn melted away, my fatigue forgotten. I'd never seen anything like it. I stepped forward and studied the body, which had belonged to a young man. It was lying in the bath, which was about a quarter full of water, stained red with blood.

'I know,' Professor Mant said, turning back to greet me and seeing the look on my face. 'Looks like he's had a PM already, albeit quite possibly the world's worst.'

The body was almost cut in two, lengthways. A huge gaping wound that ran from the throat to the pubis. The man's intestines had been pulled out and now bobbed around him in the bath like some primordial sea creature. There was nothing but a bloody stump where the man's genitals had once been. The prof pointed to the toilet and I saw the man's penis and testes floating inside, the water stained pink.

'Please tell me that the killer is in custody,' I asked, for I had never witnessed something so monstrous.

'The police have a good set of leads,' Professor Mant said. 'Someone, presumably the murderer, called 999 at 4am this morning, to give the police the location of the deceased. He was a seventeen-year-old West End sex worker who was out on the town last night with his clients; so it should be a simple process of elimination.'

Despite the grimness of the scene, I had to stifle another yawn.

'Not keeping you up, am I?' Professor Mant enquired.

I shook my head. 'It's my son,' I said. 'He's going through a phase. At least I hope that's what it is.'

I took out my notebook as Professor Mant provided a description of the scene, the man's injuries and the likely murder weapon, a Stanley knife. We found bloodstained ropes in the bedroom and an electrical cable that corresponded with whip marks on the dead man's back. He'd been tied to the bed, sodomised and whipped before being murdered.

The PM was extraordinary, partially thanks to the skill of Professor Mant in putting together what had happened, but mainly because of its sheer horror. By analysing the wounds and bloodstains, the prof worked out the order of injuries, concluding – thanks to the fact that blood had entered the lungs – that the poor man had still been conscious and breathing throughout the ordeal, only succumbing when he was stabbed in the heart. It is almost impossible to comprehend what this ordeal must have been like for the young man, reaching that point when he knew he was about to die, knowing that even the simplest pleasures and sorrows that once lay ahead of him would no longer.

Extended periods with dead bodies can invite this kind of morbid contemplation, but thankfully I never dwelled with such thoughts for too long and, with the help of the unflappable Professor Mant, who had already seen the worst of man's inhumanity in the Nazi concentration camps, we were pros through and through. Besides, the next body was already waiting – a tube jumper – and we needed to get a move on.

Cases of tube jumpers were referred to as 'one under'. Death in this manner is not instantaneous, and sometimes it goes terribly wrong. When I was at St Mary's a young woman who attempted suicide by tube was brought into casualty screaming; she'd lost her arms and legs. She screamed for death for four days before it finally came.

Although rare, it can be the case that tube jumpers fail when they leap even a fraction of a second late and hit the side of the train, falling into the gap between the train and the platform, and then rolling along as the train keeps moving. The body is twisted, and the person sometimes retains consciousness. The internal organs might be beyond repair but the twist prevents the body from haemorrhaging; sometimes the victim can even speak, but once removed from the track the body untwists and the person quickly bleeds to death. In such cases a doctor would administer a tranquilliser, while a priest was called to provide comfort if the dying person so desired.

Tube jumpers came in all shapes, ages and sizes. While I was at St Mary's, I dealt with the body of an Oxford professor who jumped in front of a train at Paddington Station. Another jumper was an ex-girlfriend of Frank Sinatra who had sought solace in London's nightlife, only to find loneliness and depression.

In this case, the victim had been decapitated, making for a relatively straightforward PM. By the time we had finished with the body, the police had their man for the murder of the sex worker: a Soho-based advertising executive who readily confessed. He explained how he had lost his temper after the young man had refused to see him again – because he was too violent. After a short hearing a few weeks later, the murderer was sent to Broadmoor – the infamous high-security psychiatric hospital in Berkshire – where he would be held indefinitely.

As the evening approached, I tackled some paperwork in my office and waited until long after dark, when I was certain the building was empty and George was in his flat, no doubt counting his ill-gotten gains. I was exhausted, but buzzing at the thought of what I might have captured on my recordings. Although this had been an extraordinarily long day, I was too excited to feel fatigued as I retrieved the devices from their hiding places in the PM room.

I removed the tiny cassettes, placed them in the Dictaphone recorder and hit play, which was when I realised that I had a lot to learn about covert recording. Over the sound of hissing static, I could make out the occasional yell of fury from Professor Johnson and the clatter of tools in the steel sink, but I could barely make out a single word of anything else, let alone a clear confession of guilt. An occasional phrase hinted at George's guilt but there was certainly nothing convincing.

I resolved to keep trying and reloaded the mini-tape recorders. I was about to head home when the phone rang. It was Dr Basil Purdue, one of the younger pathologists, who told me that the Criminal Investigation Department (CID) had called him to a 'bad one' and he needed me to come along. It was the end of what had been an extremely hot day, and Basil's car was boiling as we drove to the address in Herne Hill. Dr Purdue was recently qualified and had therefore only just been let loose on murder cases. This meant he was anxious to get everything exactly right and spent hours examining murder victims, recording every detail.

DI Baker welcomed us with the same phrase: 'It's a bad one.' As we climbed the stairs, the sweet, cloying stink of decomposition hit our nostrils. Teddy bears surrounded the pillows upon which lay the heads of a boy of five and his four-year-old sister. Dressed in clean pyjamas, they showed no external signs of trauma. The lengthy PM, performed in silence, concluded that the children's mother had fed them with weedkiller and rat poison before suffocating them with a pillow. The mother, who admitted murder, would, like the advertising executive, be sent to Broadmoor for an indefinite stay. Two monstrous crimes in just one day: both so utterly different.

DAYS PASSED IN a never-ending blur of activity. Between arriving early and leaving late to install and check my secret recordings, managing the day-to-day running of the mortuary while getting quotes for and lobbying for building improvements, as well as attending crime scenes and PMs,

I was rapidly becoming exhausted. My efforts at recording were getting better thanks to repositioning, but were still difficult to make out – let alone clear enough for a jury to be convinced that the voices heard belonged to a particular person.

A few days later, I was in early as usual, playing back the previous day's recordings in my office when a knock at the door caused me to jump out of my skin. Sweeping the tapes into my drawer, I asked whoever it was to come in and was surprised to see Sally. Sally was our newest employee, having joined us in June, a few weeks earlier. She was only eighteen years old but had so impressed me with her maturity as well as her excellent science grades that I'd hired her as a trainee mortuary technician.

'Can I have a quick word, Mr Everett?' she asked.

'Of course. How are you finding things here? No problems, I hope?'

'Well, funny you should say that,' she said, sounding uncertain. 'This is a delicate matter.'

'Do go on. Anything you say here, I'll treat in the strictest confidence.'

'Well, George, he er …'

At the mention of my deputy my ears pricked up. 'Yes, yes, please go on,' I said, trying not to sound too eager.

'Well, I overheard him talking about stealing things, and he offered me a bribe to keep my mouth shut.'

'A bribe, you say?', trying not to sound too delighted. At last, the evidence I so desperately needed! 'How much?'

'£100.'

'And what did you say?'

'I didn't know what to say at first, but then I told him to keep his money, I wouldn't say anything.'

I grabbed a piece of paper and, once I explained to Sally all that I knew and how it was important that she go with me to the police, we put pen to paper, working on a joint statement. After Sally left, I thanked her profusely, typed up our statements, transcribed my recordings and delivered them to the director of service at Southwark Council. Finally, he agreed to call the police. At long last, I had the investigation I so desperately desired!

I received a call just a few hours later to attend a meeting at Camberwell police station where I was met by the area commander, Detective Chief Superintendent (DCS) Peter Holland. Prior to his appointment, Peter had worked on the murder squad and our paths had crossed at the mortuary. He was a tenacious detective, strict but fair. Peter immediately told me that he had his own suspicions. 'I worked a murder case last year, a pub brawl that ended with a stabbing,' he said as we walked to his office. 'The murder victim had £5 in his pockets. Sometime after he arrived at the mortuary the £5 went missing!'

For the next two hours we struggled to listen to my covert recordings. Peter then decided that they should be sent to the police laboratory for enhancement. DI Ian Johnson, who would later become the chief constable of the British Transport Police, joined us. I spent a further three hours telling the officers my story, relating George's disciplinary history, and drawing accurate floor plans of the mortuary. Once all this was done, Ian told me to head back to the mortuary, and tell no one, not even my bosses, about what I'd spoken about that day, or about the police investigation. We didn't know how high up the corruption went. Peter added that CIB2 – the Met's anti-corruption squad – would be in touch in a few days' time. I returned to the mortuary, my spirits soaring.

An interesting case was waiting for me. The body of a teenage girl. Her name was Rebecca, just sixteen years old, with a single gunshot wound to her head. The bullet had passed directly through her temples. Her boyfriend, Winston, was under arrest for murder but insisted that he hadn't fired the fatal shot.

I quickly prepped the room while Professor Mant studied an X-ray of the girl's head. Doctors at King's College Hospital had tried to revive her but, as Professor Mant indicated, bullet fragments were spread throughout her brain.

While the cause of death was never in doubt, the means by which she had died was. At first, Winston had asked a friend to hide his gun, which the police later recovered. Then Winston said he had been cleaning it when it went off, but Professor Mant's PM had revealed burn marks, typical of the muzzle of the gun being placed close to the head, so unless he'd been cleaning it right by her temple, then this was impossible.

Winston then changed his story, claiming that he and Rebecca were daring each other to play Russian roulette after he put a single bullet in one of the revolver's chambers. They each had a go, but then Rebecca insisted on having another try and fired the fatal shot. There was no gun residue on

Rebecca's hands, but the murder squad knew that this story was enough to cause a jury to have reasonable doubt and to have to acquit Winston of murder. So they charged him with manslaughter and a jury sent him to prison for six years.

Soon after this case, I received a telephone call from Detective Superintendent (DSI) John Ball of CIB2. He told me to report sick at work and meet him at Scotland Yard. Known within the force as the 'rubber heels' or as 'the Ghost Squad' for the way they discreetly spied on their fellow officers suspected of corruption, CIB2 were understandably unpopular within the force and operated very much in isolation. This team of eighteen detectives had to be the best that Scotland Yard had to offer because they were trying to catch people who knew only too well how the law worked, were suspicious by nature, and were able to cover their tracks. They achieved a number of convictions, but in many cases, the miscreants were simply sacked rather than taken to a trial, to save the police force's embarrassment. Apart from this, CIB2 inspired a healthy fear that restrained those officers who might otherwise have been tempted to abuse their considerable power for financial gain.

John Ball cut a comical figure as he was desperately trying to quit smoking. To combat his addiction he chewed sweets all day long. For this reason, he was known as 'Sweetie', although no one would have ever dared to say it to his face. The squad was secretly running a book on when he would succumb and finally take a drag, but for now at least, the sweets seemed to be working – although they were doing nothing for his teeth or his waistline.

DSI Ball took me to the squad room. 'We're already inves-
tigating 43 suspect coroner's officers across London,' he told
me as he pointed to their names, written neatly on huge
blackboards, alongside their suspected crimes. One corrupt
officer was bad enough, but 43!

'We are aware of corruption within your division,
Peter,' he continued, chewing on a wine gum as I studied
the names and their suspected crimes, 'but the fact that your
own mortuary staff are corrupt has opened a new avenue of
investigation.'

I agreed to gather intelligence and be the squad's eyes
and ears on the ground. Each evening, after everyone had
left for the night, I would check the coroner's officers' waste
bins and search their desks, but we were dealing with highly
experienced police officers who were well versed in counter-
surveillance methods. Ball then asked me if I was prepared to
take on a more proactive role in the investigation.

'I'll do anything,' I said, 'as long as we can clean up my
mortuary.'

Had I known what was to follow, I might not have been
so bold.

6

The tragedy of terror

July 1982

Of course, death waits for no one. While I tried to remain patient until the next part of the police investigation could get underway, bodies continued to arrive at the mortuary in a steady stream. Late one afternoon, I was interrupted in my attempts to make headway through Himalayan piles of paperwork in my office by the arrival of the body of a young Jamaican woman.

Julia, who had died aged 35, was well-nourished, and there were no obvious marks that suggested the cause of death but, confronted with an array of familiar symptoms, the doctors at Guy's Hospital had written 'suspected drugs overdose' on the admission form. The PM was booked in for the following morning but I was especially concerned, because this was no ordinary overdose.

The detective accompanying the body had arrived with an agent from HM Customs and Excise Drugs Investigation Unit, Clive, a short man with a crisp Etonian accent dressed in a tailored suit. He was based across the river from Southwark Mortuary in Custom House on Lower Thames Street.

Customs had had an office there far longer than Southwark had had its mortuary, ever since the 15th century in fact, which just goes to show that while death and taxes can't be avoided, our rulers are far more concerned about the latter than the former. This despite the fact that plenty of people have died in Customs House thanks to several explosions of alcohol and gunpowder through the centuries: two popular imports that were inspected in the candle-lit building until the early decades of the 20th century. By the 1980s, however, it was home to the Investigation and Intelligence Department of Her Majesty's Customs and Excise, and this included their drugs squad.

'An early morning commuter found her,' Clive said, 'unconscious and leant up against a wall in a side street close to London Bridge station. No coat, no wallet, nothing to identify her, no jewellery or papers of any kind. After the doctors watched her die, unable to do anything to save her, they called the cops and the cops called me.'

'How on earth did you identify her?' I asked.

'A young lady with no ID and dead of a massive overdose means one thing to me: a drugs mule. And they often come from Jamaica. I checked her photograph with the flight crews who flew from Jamaica yesterday. A couple of them recognised her. The mules tend to stand out a bit. They travel alone and refuse food and water. Once I had a seat number, I had her name so asked the Jamaican police to check with her family and here we are.'

Julia had, according to her family back in Jamaica, been a cocaine mule for quite some time. Her plan had been to save up to escape the gang-ravaged slums of Kingston for the UK with her two sons, aged eight and ten. They would now be raised by their grandparents which meant, as these grandparents aged and became too old to take care of them, that they were in danger of becoming so-called 'yardies'.

The term 'yardie' was a name used to describe the bored young men who hung about in the back yards in the slums of Kingston. These slums had grown in the wake of British decolonisation. When the occupiers left for good in 1962, they took the infrastructure with them – teachers, doctors, administrators, police officers, court officials, etc. Subsequent years of social mismanagement, along with political violence, caused the rich–poor divide to widen and the slums to grow. Many young Jamaicans left their homes to find work in the UK and sent their wages home to their families, with the hope of escaping the slums, often leaving their children in the care of grandparents. Many stayed for far longer than they intended, and soon the ageing grandparents found themselves unable to cope with teenage grandchildren who were tempted to join in with the growing get-rich-quick drugs trade and/or with the violent struggle for power between the main two political parties. These children never really grew up, and often adopted a live-fast-die-young attitude that became the yardie hallmark. Over the coming years, yardies would begin to arrive in the UK, looking to make their fortunes in its lucrative drug trade, and their arrival coincided with Southwark seeing an incredible upsurge in the number of shootings and stabbings.

'She'd make about £1,000 per trip,' Clive said, nodding down at the body, 'but it comes with a lot of risk. Even swallowing the packages is dangerous. They'll be packed into lozenges of some sort, using condoms and cling film usually, compressed and heat-sealed. You dip it in olive oil, place it in your mouth and gulp. It has to be done with conviction every time – any hesitancy and the package might get caught and you'll choke to death. And then you wash it all down with a large dose of constipating agent. An attack of the nerves can be disastrous on the ten-hour flight from Kingston to London.'

'And then there's the journey itself. You'll receive a long prison sentence if you're caught or, well, here's the perfect example of just how powerful the stomach's acids are.'

Clive was part of a new team set up by Customs to try to disrupt the use of mules, so much so that people would start to see it less as an opportunity than as a one-way ticket to hell. In fact, they even put up a poster at Kingston's airport which read: 'Drug mules beware: it's a plane ticket to hell'. But a lack of money and staff meant that the Jamaican authorities were only able to arrest one mule a day; they believed that on certain flights the number of mules was as high as eight out of every ten passengers. In one surprise sweep at Heathrow airport, everyone on a flight from Kingston was searched and X-rayed for cocaine. Twenty-three swallowers were discovered, including two children. One week later a further nineteen were caught on a BA flight from Jamaica into Gatwick.

'Even if just one in ten passengers is attempting to smuggle drugs, that's say, conservatively speaking, twenty kilos a flight,' Clive explained. 'There are four flights a day from Jamaica to the UK, flying five times a week, 50 weeks a year. A kilo of coke in the UK that's already been cut is worth more than £60,000, so we're talking about twenty tonnes of coke worth £1.2 billion arriving in the UK via people like Julia.'

According to her family, Julia had planned another two trips; she'd calculated that once they were done she'd have enough to start a new life with her boys in the UK.

While this story was indeed heartbreaking, I had a more immediate problem. George was in the building. This young woman still had tens of thousands of pounds worth of cocaine inside her. If George found out, I was sure that he'd have no trouble 'preparing' the body for the PM that evening, making off with the drugs. After all, he'd been in trouble before for opening up the body of a murder victim before the police had arrived. All he'd received as punishment was a limp slap on the wrist. What was that compared to the possible reward of tens of thousands of pounds in drug money?

There was nothing else I could do, however, for even if I were able to explain my impossible-to-prove suspicions to Clive and the detective, there was nowhere else for Julia's body to go. So once the relevant forms had been filled out and the body had been placed in a fridge, I brought my mountains of paperwork down to the PM room, took a seat at one of the counters and worked late into the night, guarding Julia's body.

There is perhaps no quieter place in which to work. After a while I could hear my own heartbeat and, as the various forms were completed and filed neatly away through a fug of tiredness, I couldn't help but think of a quote from Yeats. 'Why should we honour only those that die upon the field of battle? A man may show as reckless a courage in entering into the abyss of himself.' Alone with all that paperwork, with no one but the dead for company, I felt pretty close to the abyss that night, I can tell you.

I NEVER FELT uncomfortable when alone in the mortuary at night. After all, it's not the dead that one has to fear, it's the living, and a mortuary building, as secure as it is, and unlikely as it is to attract murderers, is probably one of the safest places on the planet. I did often wonder about an afterlife, however, and would ask myself, when looking at the bodies, where did 'they' go? As in, where did that part of them that made them 'them' when they were alive go? I would often arrive home late at night and upon stepping into the bedroom I'd 'sense' that Wendy was there, even though the room was pitch black and she wasn't making a sound. In the mortuary at 2am with the lights off, I could sense nothing. All these bodies had been emptied of – for want of a better word – their soul, their energy. I had heard of experiments where people who died on a bed rigged to a set of sensitive scales had lost two ounces in weight at the moment they passed. I'm not religious in the slightest, but I like to think that the 'energy' that keeps us alive and represents who we are as an active being is somehow returned to the universe when we die.

As for death itself, I'm not afraid of dying in the slightest. I look forward to it in fact; it's life's last great adventure. After seeing the myriad ways people's lives come to an unpleasant end, however, I'm more concerned with the form it might take.

EVENTUALLY, ON THIS particular evening, having reached the end of my own 'heroic' attempts at endurance, I was forced to abandon my post and slope off to bed, hoping against hope that George hadn't found out or been tipped off by someone who'd overheard or seen Clive the Customs officer and put two and two together.

It felt as though my head had just hit the pillow when the alarm rang. It was barely light outside. I wanted to be early, so quickly showered and dressed and lit my pipe on the way, walking at a fast clip the short distance to the mortuary. To my relief, Julia's body was intact and so I waited in the PM room until Professor Johnson arrived, along with Clive, Cliff the lab liaison officer and the detective.

When Julia's body was at last opened, we all crowded around, keen to know what was inside. Professor Johnson pulled a 22-centimetre-long condom, about eight centimetres in diameter, from Julia's stomach. It was packed with cocaine. As we studied it, it seemed to us as though it was intact. Professor Johnson then pulled out a second condom, the same size. This one had a hole in it.

'The stomach's acids dissolve condoms,' the Customs officer said. 'It's a race against time with such a long flight.'

We weighed the packages, and Clive estimated they were worth more than £100,000. George didn't appear until much later that day, and I made sure I was the one to tell him what had happened since his last shift, just so I could see the pain of a golden opportunity missed cross his face.

After this, it was time for me to go on a short holiday. I left the building with a smile on my face and the hope that when I returned, the end of George's criminal reign would not be far off.

BY TRADITION, IN the third week of July, my parents would come down from Yorkshire and have a mini holiday. We would start each day with a visit to Regent's Park and watch the military band play through a series of favourite popular pieces from musicals and operas and so on. This year, however, my parents were unable to make the journey, so Wendy and I travelled up to Yorkshire.

I soon found myself back on Saltburn beach, relaxing in a deckchair, soaking up the sun where, all those years ago I'd first laid eyes on a dead body. It was a lovely afternoon, the sea was almost still, seagulls wheeled overhead, swooping down to catch chips tossed into the sky by holidaymakers, when I caught the faint sound of a portable radio being carried past. A programme had been interrupted by a newsflash, and I caught the words 'IRA bomb', 'fatalities' and 'London's' something or other. I scrambled out of the deckchair, quickly ran over to the young man who was holding the radio and asked if I could listen in. IRA terrorists had blown up the bandstand at Regent's Park on the very day we should have been there.

This was the second of two bombs. The first, comprising eleven kilograms of gelignite and fourteen kilograms of nails, had exploded in the boot of a blue Morris Marina parked on South Carriage Drive in Hyde Park just as soldiers of the Household Cavalry, Queen Elizabeth II's official bodyguard regiment, were performing their daily Changing of the Guard procession. Seven guardsmen were killed.

The second attack happened when a bomb exploded underneath a bandstand in Regent's Park. Thirty military bandsmen of the Royal Green Jackets were on the stand performing music from *Oliver!* to a crowd of 120 people. Three soldiers were killed outright, while a fourth, their standard-bearer, died from his wounds three days later. Other soldiers in the procession were badly wounded, and a number of civilians were injured.

Quickly donning my clothes, I rushed to the high street in search of a phone.

We always had to be prepared as, in a city like London, it was never a question of 'if' but 'when'. To that end we checked the major incident store weekly (this was where we kept dozens of body bags, stretchers and other basic mortuary equipment that could be quickly retrieved in the wake of a disaster), and I regularly briefed staff on our plans. After a major incident like this terrorist bombing, dozens of orders must be actioned within a matter of minutes. The coroner's court was designated as a control centre for fatalities, with rooms for police liaison officers and provision for interviewing relatives. St George's churchyard backed onto the mortuary complex and would be used to house several large marquees containing equipment, personnel and facilities.

Professor Johnson answered my call; the police had been trying to locate me but I'd been unreachable, on the beach all day with Wendy, my son and my parents. This left me in a predicament. Although our major incident plan did not need to go into action in this instance as there was just enough room in London's mortuaries that day (at this time they regularly ran overcapacity, but we were lucky on this occasion), four bodies had been taken to Southwark and were awaiting PMs.

'The forensic teams are here already,' Professor Johnson told me.

'I'm 300 miles away,' I said. 'I'll set off now, but it'll take me six hours to get back. You'll have to start without me, and I'll check everything off as soon as I get there.'

I grabbed my things, apologised to Wendy and my parents and caught the first available train back to London. By the time I arrived that evening, all of the examinations were over.

Most of the men that were killed had been in their twenties; two were just nineteen and one of these, Lance Corporal Jeffrey Young, had a baby daughter. Two others had been married for less than a month.

Professor Johnson was exhausted, physically and emotionally. 'A Corporal came to identify the bodies,' he told me as I started checking the paperwork. 'He marched into the mortuary and saluted each victim before marching out again.'

No one has ever been charged with the Regent's Park bombing, and Gilbert McNamee, convicted of making the Hyde Park bomb, was released after serving twelve years of a 25-year sentence under the terms of the Good Friday Agreement. His conviction was later quashed after the fingerprint evidence used to convict him was called into question. The trial of a second man collapsed in 2014, but Lance Corporal Jeffrey Young's daughter is still hoping to bring a civil case against this suspect.

Seven horses were killed, and the pictures of the horses' corpses lying among the debris became one of the enduring images of the Troubles. One horse, Sefton, became a national icon and symbol of hope after recovering from 34 injuries and an eight-hour operation. He even returned to military service for a further two years and lived until 1993. His rider, Michael Pedersen, who was injured, also became a national hero but, tragically, revealing how such attacks have long-lasting and sometimes disastrous consequences, he took his own life and those of his two children in 2012.

SHORTLY AFTER THIS dreadful day was concluded, DSI Ball phoned: 'Make an excuse and meet me at the Yard.'

Once I arrived, Ball enthusiastically explained his idea: 'I'd like you to invite George out for a drink. Give him the impression that you've changed your mind about him, that you'd like to bury the hatchet. We'll wire you for sound and hopefully he'll start boasting to you about his crimes, maybe even try to bribe you again.'

The only place I wanted to bury the hatchet was in George's skull. However, I pushed aside visions of the miscreant laid out on the PM table with an axe in his head and readily agreed. Anything to get rid of George, although the superintendent's plan did make me feel a little nervous. I expressed concern that I wasn't a trained detective.

'There's nothing to it,' he said confidently. 'Just be yourself, and besides, you won't be in any danger. We'll make sure there're detectives all over the place.'

Of course, it was never going to be that simple.

7

Going undercover

August 1982

Keeping the investigation secret from everyone while trying to manage the mortuary and play a key role in the police operation played havoc with my personal and professional life. I arrived and left home in the small hours (usually after an interrupted night, thanks to my baby son), either because I'd been called out or because I wanted to check recordings or search for clues. I was exhausted, but at the same time I was determined to expose the corruption. As if I didn't have enough to deal with, the mortuary was in desperate need of updating. Wooden storage cupboards were rotting, aluminium sinks were rusting and bodies were literally piling up around us. Asbestos was found in the fridge doors, forcing us into emergency shutdown until they could be removed and replaced. Tempers were frayed and arguments became inevitable amid such chaos.

Until the start of the police investigation, the only way I managed to get at George was via the record player I kept in the PM room. As soon as I learned that George hated opera, I made sure Wagner's fifteen-hour epic opera, *Ring Cycle*, was on constant repeat.

We were about to start the PM of a murdered homeless man and I'd just put 'Ride of the Valkyries' on the turntable. George, who'd been skulking at the back of the PM room, left immediately. 'Works like a charm,' I muttered to myself as I placed the buckets on the PM table. I stopped when I sensed I was being looked at. I enjoyed Wagner, and I thought the profs all did too, but Professor Johnson had had enough. 'Everett, if I have to listen to another bar of Wagner I shall defenestrate the damn record player!' So I switched to Gilbert and Sullivan which the prof quite enjoyed and which George hated all the more, even when I played 'A Policeman's Lot is Not a Happy One'.

A few hours later, Mant, Johnson and I were in full blown 'discussions' about our working conditions when we were silenced by the news that a nurse had leapt from the sixth floor of St Thomas' Hospital clutching her daughters, aged three and one, and their remains were on their way to the mortuary. Their bodies were so broken it was like trying to move jelly. A specialist was called in to use various formulae to help align injuries with circumstances, to establish whether the family had jumped, or could have been pushed, or fallen. The nurse had indeed jumped but as to why, no one would ever know.

It was just as I had finished tidying up after this heartbreaking PM when DSI Ball called, asking me to meet him at the Yard. Anything to escape the particularly sombre mood this case had brought to the mortuary, which was normally, contrary to popular belief, quite a lively, even jolly, place.

WE STUDIED MAPS of London and decided that the sting should take place at the Dickens Inn in St Katharine's Dock, a short distance from the Tower of London. Having agreed on a venue, we drove down to the dock and Ball selected a table. It was duly reserved, along with the four surrounding tables, which would be filled with twelve plain-clothed officers from CIB2. All that remained was for me to entice the deputy into the trap. Returning to the Yard, I telephoned George and invited him out for a drink. This unexpected request threw him off guard. No doubt hoping that his boss had finally seen the light, he readily agreed.

That evening, I walked the short distance to Guy's Hospital car park for my rendezvous with an officer from the Yard's technical section. My apprehension only increased when I spotted a yellow British Telecom van weaving its way rapidly towards me. It couldn't have looked more like a sur-veillance van if it had tried. Its roof bristled with a ridiculous array of aerials in all shapes and sizes. The driver, squashed into his seat, his head bowed so he could see out of the win-dow, was huge and couldn't have looked more like a police officer. I climbed into the van's interior where a technician was waiting to fit me with a transmitter and recording device. The battery pack, which was the size of a brick, was taped to the base of my spine while the microphone attached to the inside of my jacket sleeve. 'It's hardly discreet, is it?' I asked. 'I wouldn't exactly describe it as a "hidden" recording device.'

'You just be careful with it, sir,' the technician said curtly. 'Break this and that's half of our annual budget gone. And don't be fooled into thinking that all those detectives are there to protect you tonight; they're there to make sure nothing happens to this. Just make sure your jacket doesn't get caught on it and don't let the suspect get behind you or put his hand on your back.'

With those words of encouragement and advice, and feeling about as adept at undercover work as Inspector Clouseau, I set off on my mission, walking the short distance to George's flat, trying to keep my heart rate under 200 beats per minute. The adrenaline was really pumping, and by the time I'd climbed the stairs I'd started to perspire excessively. I stopped to wipe the sweat from my face. If George exposed this plan, then God knows what would happen. At the very least I'd end up with a pair of black eyes and he would probably follow that up by suing me, the Metropolitan Police and Southwark Council. I had visions of George retiring to the Bahamas with the payout.

George threw open the door the moment I knocked, causing me to step back in surprise.

'You look hot, mate,' George said, shaking my hand as if we were long-lost friends. 'You should take off your jacket.'

'I'm alright, it's just the stairs,' I said quickly. 'It's cool enough outside.'

George was dressed in a suit and tie and was wearing enough aftershave for an entire rugby squad. I immediately started to feel queasy, thinking that after George had found out (this now felt like an inevitability) I would be unceremoniously fired from the service for my baseless subterfuge. My fears of discovery were compounded a few seconds later, when after having only walked a few metres down the road, the yellow BT van drove past us.

'What the hell's that thing?' George asked.

'What?' I replied, pretending not to have noticed.

'That van with all the things sticking out of its roof. Never seen anything like it before.'

I shrugged and started talking about work, which took George's mind off the van but, a few seconds later, DSI Ball drove past in his Rover. George clocked him straight away.

'That guy's a cop!' he said.

'What?'

'That guy in the silver Rover, he's a cop. I've seen him down the mortuary before.'

Inwardly I was cursing my luck, by now thinking that things had started badly and were likely to get worse before long. Outwardly I adapted the air of a man entirely at ease with the world and pointed out that it was only natural for the Super to pass by this way as Tower Bridge's nick was just up the road from us. This seemed to allay George somewhat, but he now seemed to be on alert, keeping a careful eye on everything around us.

I almost groaned when we entered the Dickens Inn. It was busy with post-work drinkers, but even I could see that the twelve detectives sent to watch over me didn't know the difference between 'plain-clothed' and 'not looking like cops'.

It was so obvious to me; they were all male, all had neat and tidy short hair, pressed jeans, were roughly the same age and all of them seemed to have only half an eye on their made-up conversations, like the extras on *EastEnders*. After collecting our drinks from the bar, we weaved our way through the crowds to our table.

Amazingly, George seemed entirely oblivious and obviously felt completely safe now we were in the pub. He started to talk straight away, offering me the chance to get in on the action, naming all the other corrupt officers he knew about while detailing their modus operandi, and repeating the allegations he'd made against the pathologists and the hospital administrators: that they knew about the thefts and were taking cuts. I pretended to consider, explaining my reservations, saying I was finding it difficult to believe that it was all as easy and carefree as George had indicated. This only fired George up to new and dizzying heights of boasting about how easy it all was and how much money we could make. He described how he and other technicians illegally sold brains to medical schools, while eyes were sold (if they were quick enough, for they had to be fresh) for corneal grafting. Pituitary glands went to commercial medical research companies who used them to manufacture growth hormones for underdeveloped children, and temporal bones were sold to otorhinolaryngologists (ear, nose and throat) surgeons for practice. The drinks came in quick succession and, by the time we were on our fourth pint, the booze was really starting to get the better of me. During a brief lull in George's boasting, his mood suddenly changed. He frowned at me through the fog of four pints of Stella, leaned forward and accused me of taping the conversation.

By now, emboldened by the alcohol, I had no trouble dealing with this accusation. I leapt to my feet, partially opened my jacket and – I could see the undisguised horror on the officers' faces behind George – demanded that George search me, while accusing him of outrageous and insulting behaviour.

George collapsed back into his chair and apologised. 'Sorry, mate,' he said. 'It's just you were so dead set against the whole thing.'

'Never mind,' I said. 'Let's have another drink and forget all about it.'

For three hours, George talked non-stop, all of it filling the reel after reel of tape in the little yellow van. Vino veritas was certainly working, but it was also affecting me. I was so inebriated I forgot that the other detectives were there and that we had a plan. I was now enjoying my role so much that I readily agreed when George suggested we repair to the Tower Hotel for a meal. I have no memory of that meal whatsoever, but when we finally parted company and I weaved my way off Tower Bridge Road to get to my apartment, a car screeched to a halt beside me and four CIB officers bundled me into the back of it. A few minutes later we arrived at the Yard's underground car park from which I was half carried to the squad room and dumped in a chair.

'You did it, Peter!' Ball said, delighted.

'Did I?' I replied, the room spinning before me, now on the verge of nausea.

'You bloody did! He named names, told you everything they did and how they did it. You were marvellous.'

'I was?' I had no idea. A pot of coffee and a mug was thrust before me.

'Yes, the way you led him on, promising not to say anything and then asking for a piece of the action. That was great!'

'Oh, right, erm …'

'And when he accused you of taping. Magnificent!'

'Excuse me,' I said, unable to absorb any further compliments, 'but can someone please direct me to the nearest lavatory?'

After some alone time in the bathroom, and two pots of coffee, I was debriefed and driven home where I was told to wait for a call the next day.

By the time I staggered through the front door it was hardly worth going to bed. Wendy was up with the baby and, seeing and smelling the state of me, she opened her mouth to tell me off. I held up my hands. 'It's not what you think!' I said quickly, going on to confess. I hadn't told Wendy about the police operation because I hadn't wanted to worry her.

The next morning I reported sick, wondering whether George's hangover was as bad as mine. Ball collected me from my home and drove me to the Yard for a working breakfast. We listened to over four hours of tapes, all relating to the previous evening; I hoped they would never be used in court as I found parts of the conversation quite embarrassing, particularly those sections where I expressed a desire to join George's operation and, later, my words slurring as I encouraged George to tell me more. If you ever want to be put off drinking, you should get someone to tape you when you're drunk. Played back when sober, you sound like the world's stupidest, most unattractive and boring person.

By the time all of this was done, it was lunch. Ball suggested we go to the Tank (Scotland Yard's bar). I wasn't ready to be confronted by even the sight of more alcohol, and was about to suggest a cafe when the duty officer interrupted us to say that Sally had called. George had suddenly become suspicious, perhaps he'd even been tipped off by one of his bent cops, and had locked her out of the mortuary. Realising he was probably destroying important evidence to avoid arrest, the team jumped in four squad cars, and fifteen minutes later we pulled up in Guy's Hospital car park, just around the corner from the mortuary. Ball decided that I should enter the mortuary and assess the situation; if I spotted anything untoward I was to appear at the door and produce the time-honoured signal of scratching my nose and the squad would make the arrests there and then. I duly went, but once I arrived at the mortuary not only could I find no sign of George, but no sign of any tampering either. Ball was halfway through a packet of Chewitts when I reappeared and gave him the bad news. After a few thoughtful chews, Ball made his decision: 'Sod it, we practically have a confession. Let's nick him.'

We waited until George and Eric the assistant reappeared at the mortuary, at which point they were immediately arrested, handcuffed and removed to Cannon Row station for questioning. Sally and I joined the remaining squad in the PM room and, much to the amusement of Dr West, who'd just finished a PM on a shotgun suicide, we started searching for evidence. He even offered to open the fridge doors for the team, in case George had squirrelled away something next to the suicide victim. He received no takers, but I thought it wasn't a bad suggestion, so I took up the offer but found nothing. We were looking for anything that suggested wrongdoing, such as stolen items or paperwork that would implicate favouritism towards certain funeral directors, or anything that George might have collected as insurance against any coroner's officers and funeral directors, in case they developed cold feet about committing their alleged crimes or were arrested and threatened to give evidence against George.

As we carried on rummaging through the PM room, Sally mentioned that she had seen one of the coroner's officers going into the basement area. There were only two things in the basement: the records and the incinerator. Dashing downstairs, I opened the incinerator door. Small bits of burned paper fluttered around in the hearth. Some of it still had legible writing. It was sent it off to the laboratory, where Ball hoped that the scientists would be able decipher the charred remains.

OF COURSE, THE mortuary still needed managing in the midst of all this and now, without my deputy and his assistant, Sally and I were up against it. My bosses, who I felt should have been shaking my hand and patting me on the back, expressed only annoyance that the mortuary had been exposed as a hotbed of criminal activity and was now, thanks to George's arrest, in disarray. They demanded that I make sure that there was no impact on the day-to-day running of the mortuary. I was already at the edge of exhaustion and needed to rest, but the pressure only continued to increase. They made the point that death rates had fallen dramatically in recent months.

We had always had seasonal fluctuations, with winter being the busy season, but this was different. The fall-off was thanks to the Second World War. Had those people killed in the conflict lived to a ripe old age, they would have been dying in the 1980s. On the other hand, the murder rate had gone dramatically up over the past year or so, and its upward curve showed no signs of diminishing. As Southwark was a forensic mortuary, we were busier than any other. It was around this time that we dealt with an exceedingly complex murder case which went something like this:

Tony moved to London where he met and fell in love with Jane, whom he married a year later. Following three months of wedded bliss, Jane met and fell for a woman called Caroline. Tony accepted this adulterous relationship and Caroline moved in with the couple. A few weeks later, Tony met a man by the name of Patrick, and they too started an affair. Jane accepted Tony's adultery and Patrick moved in. So the four lovers all shared the same flat. Some kind of bliss existed for a few months until Mary (whose birth name was Dave) arrived on the scene and started affairs with Jane and Caroline. Having had enough of this complicated set up, Tony and Patrick moved into a second flat in Brixton. A few weeks after this, Tony announced to Patrick that he was going to move back in with Jane (and Caroline and Mary). Patrick took this news badly and an argument ensued which ended with Tony being stabbed to death. Patrick was so overcome with remorse that he hung himself while in Brixton Prison. For a week, we found ourselves in the unusual position of having the two lovers, murderer and victim, side by side in the same refrigerator, despite having died separated by space and time.

WHEN I WASN'T at the mortuary, I was with Ball and his team at the Yard, where I helped them collate every bit of information in the case against George and Eric. We listened to the tapes countless times and read dozens of statements. The squad had carried out an extensive investigation; funeral directors, coroner's officers and relatives of the deceased had all made statements. A funeral director reported that George had offered him cheap second-hand coffins. One of the coroner's officers had asked an undertaker to sponsor him for membership of a Masonic Lodge; the undertaker refused. Consequently, the coroner's officer ceased his preferential treatment and the lucrative trade in body removals. In revenge, when the police moved, this undertaker was the first to turn whistle-blower.

Ball's operation was supposed to expand into North London, but his bosses pulled the plug. Two years previously Operation Countryman had resulted in massive embarrassment for the force. This investigation into police corruption (which found corruption to be widespread throughout the force) had involved dozens of police officers, cost £4 million but led to zero convictions. It did cause 250 police officers to resign, however. The Met management did not want to have to deal with another huge scandal but, by the time George and Eric's pre-trial hearing came up at Bow Street, 43 serving police officers were already under investigation, with three of my own officers committed for trial (posh Ted, fat Frank and Martin, a thin, miserable man who I rarely saw at work). If I had thought that the police operation to catch George had been hairy, that was nothing compared to my appearance as the star witness in a trial that would, to my great surprise, grip the nation.

8

The trial

January 1983

Confronted with the recording, George had decided to plead guilty. Eric, on the other hand, continued to insist on his innocence and so he had to face a trial by jury.

At first, I had approached the corruption trial as just another case; after all, I was quite used to the workings of the justice system. But as the trial began, and I was placed in the witness's waiting room, it was quite a different story. The many other witnesses (mainly friends of George) all gave me daggers, muttering between themselves. What they were saying I could only imagine, but I am certain they would have liked nothing better than to have seen my body lying on the mortuary slab.

When John Ball dropped by to say hello and saw what was going on, he pulled me up and escorted me from the room.

'We can't leave you here,' he said, speaking through a half-chewed Toffo and, after some discussion, I was allowed to wait in a small office used by the police officers who worked at the court.

A multitude of TV crews and Fleet Street's finest were already outside the building, fighting for a prime position. I knew, with what I planned to say, that I was going to be the star of the show, not a position I revelled in in the slightest. My desire to appear in the glow of the theatrical footlights had long since vanished, and I longed for the relative peace and quiet of the mortuary.

Finally, a loud voice boomed: 'Call Peter Everett!' and I entered stage right to begin the most important performance of my life.

I wasn't nervous about giving evidence in court; after all, I'd done nothing wrong and I'd seen many court cases by this time, but the sight of journalists crammed into the press box, overflowing into the public gallery, did cause me to break into a sweat. The remaining places in the public gallery seemed to be taken up by grave-faced members of the guild of morticians. They did not look pleased to see me. Also present were Eric's parents, convinced of his innocence. I was sorry that they had to go through such a dreadful experience but, in my opinion, their son was 100 per cent guilty of stealing from the dead.

I was used to the ancient, pokey courtrooms of the Old Bailey but Southwark was no better – even worse, in fact. To my surprise, I found that the witness box sat directly in front of the Judge. I could have touched him on the nose. More disconcertingly, I could also have touched George and Eric, who were immediately adjacent to my position. They were both trying and failing not to glare at me as if they wanted me to drop dead of a heart attack.

The judge, Edward Fox – an elderly man, softly spoken with gold-rimmed glasses – perhaps sensing my nervousness, did his best to put me at ease by explaining my role in the case, the difficult position I had found myself in and that this trial was absolutely necessary. He then issued me with a judge's warning, an unusual edict that protects the witness from being forced to reveal anything outside of the public's knowledge, or saying anything that would implicate them in a crime. Ball later explained that this was introduced as a cautionary measure in case Eric's lawyer tried to distract from the purpose of the trial by attempting to incriminate me. Apparently, in the audio recording made with George at the Dickens Inn, my efforts to make the deputy reveal more about his various 'fiddles', it sounded as if I was ready to collude with him. Besides, I was not the one on trial here, even though I soon felt like it.

And so, with a deep breath, I began. My evidence lasted two days and, between all the crimes I described, I took every opportunity to expose the archaic system and conditions in which mortuary staff worked. We desperately needed reform and renovation.

Eric's defence was based on the fact that he'd only ever received semi-legitimate payments made to mortuary staff, the kind of payments that everyone else took. I explained that mortuary staff received so-called 'coroner's fees' from the pathologist for each case they assisted on (always paid in cash), for preparing and dissecting the body in advance so that the pathologist could be in and out and on to the next body as quickly as possible, not wasting any time. This was common practice, if unregulated, throughout the country and could only be called semi-legitimate at best.

Similarly, funeral directors also paid a fee for measuring the body. Without the mortuary staff's cooperation, funeral directors would have to waste time and manpower sending someone down to measure up so that they knew what coffin to bring. It was far easier to tip the mortuary staff to do this for them. This was also paid in cash and a common and accepted practice, if unregulated.

I saw the faces of my fellow guild members pale as I explained this system and as they saw the journalists carefully recording my every word. The taxman would be listening!

I then explained why it was so easy for corruption to exist in the UK's mortuaries.

'There is no statutory control over the running of the mortuaries,' I explained. 'Local district authorities, under the Public Health Act of 1926 must provide a place to receive corpses and perform post-mortem examinations. The Health and Safety Commission inspects hygiene standards, but we haven't had an inspection in years and the mortuary is in a terribly outdated state. Meanwhile, coroners are paid by county councils and answerable to the Home Office; pathologists are employees of the National Health Service; while coroner's officers are police officers. This unregulated set up, with no public body in overall control, leaves it open to abuse.'

The prosecutor then asked me about illegal payments to mortuary staff; this was the opportunity I had been waiting for. I went into detail about the black market for organs: eyes sold to Middle Eastern patients through a Harley Street clinic, brains sent to anatomy departments and pituitary glands sold to drug companies for research and to produce growth hormones – all without family permission.

'In fact,' I said, warming to my role, as I saw that I had the complete attention of the entire court, 'the dead do not rest in peace, but in pieces!'

AT THE END of the first day's evidence I left the court, walking hurriedly past a row of flashing cameras and journalists shouting questions, and jogged as quickly as possible away from the court and down Battle Bridge Lane, grateful to have a less than five-minute walk home.

'Peter, you're all over the news!' Wendy exclaimed as I came in the door.

I poured a gin and tonic and settled down for the 5.40pm ITN news. Sure enough, I was the lead item on all the early evening news bulletins and then again for the late evening news. The following morning I was on the front page of *The Times*. It was that 'rest in pieces' phrase that had done it, and sure enough, sensationalism overtook the trial from that moment on. Although Eric was in the dock, the media continued to focus its attention on me. The secrets of the house of the dead were on public display for the first time and the press were having a field day.

Indeed, day two was more spectacular.

'Cash and jewellery were stripped from bodies by these two unscrupulous assistants,' Frances Evans, the prosecution lawyer outlined, trying to paint George and Eric as a modern-day Burke and Hare (the infamous grave robbers who, in 1828, murdered sixteen people in order to sell their bodies to the medical profession for anatomical study).

'No sooner had undertakers delivered the corpses than their pockets were rifled and rings and watches removed. This is a rather bizarre and horrible story… They stole from families with little or no family concern.'

I then described the thefts of cash, jewellery and coffins (which were saved from crematoria furnaces and resold to different families) and explained how the police investigation had revealed that the corruption was not limited to Southwark, that thefts were taking place all over the country. I wasn't able to go into any specific detail, alas, as that was not the focus of this trial.

George, having pled guilty, then confessed to his crimes, explaining how he often removed property from highly decomposed bodies because generally speaking, that meant they'd died alone and so had no one to check on them. He explained how the system was so corrupt that he was taking in so much money he thought he was going to become a millionaire.

Up until this point, the trial had been going well for the prosecution. And then, on the afternoon of the second day, disaster struck.

I was under cross-examination. Eric's barrister, a relatively young man compared to every other legal eagle in the court, was trying to make his client seem like an innocent patsy who was a bit hapless and couldn't have been wise to all that was going on. As the lawyer finished illustrating this concept, he asked me an almost a throwaway question.

'Do you think that the man accused in the dock before you is a committed thief, guilty of the offences?'

I knew that Eric was just a teenager who'd made a stupid mistake while under George's influence, but as to his guilt, of that there was no question. My plan was to say: 'I don't *think* he's guilty, I *know* he's guilty!' but I only got as far as 'I don't think he's guilty—' before the lawyer interrupted me.

'Thankyouthatwillbeall!'

'But wait, I—'

'Mr Everett,' the judge said, interceding. 'You may stand down.'

His look told me that I'd fallen for one of the oldest tricks in the legal profession; my reply had been cut short to suit the defence.

I left the court in a depressed state at my schoolboy error; I had failed to reflect properly on the question and think carefully about my answer before opening my mouth. The jury found Eric not guilty. Ball, furious with me, stormed off without a word, his mouth stuffed full of Liquorice Allsorts.

Back at home I slumped in front of the TV, exhausted and not just a little disappointed in myself, but perked up a bit as the news that evening, even more sensationalist, seemed to be more interested in the lack of regulation and nationwide corruption than Eric's guilt or innocence. The following morning's papers really went to town on George, with head-lines such as: 'The Scandal of Gem Thefts From The Dead', 'Ghoul Stole From The Dead' and 'Mortuary Workers Rob Corpses'.

George had pled guilty to conspiracy to steal and theft. At his sentencing, Judge Edward Fox said: 'These are very grave offences,' and I'm not sure to this day whether he knew he was making a pun or not. George was given eighteen months, nine of which were suspended.

I had finally been able expose the mortuary's archaic sys-tem, as well as the nationwide corruption, and my hopes rose at the thought that this would mean change for the better, perhaps with myself at the forefront of reform.

Oh, how naive I was.

THE UK's MORTUARY system, having operated for decades practically unchecked was now suddenly in total turmoil. Stories of abuses, corruption and downright stupidity started to emerge. Several hospitals (including Peterborough District and Belfast City) had sent wrong bodies to be cremated, while Bristol Mortuary had repeatedly 'lost' people's internal organs and Sheffield Mortuary had illegally supplied uni-versities with body parts. In East Surrey Hospital one body declared dead experienced a resurrection and woke up in the fridge. In London, a senior pathologist had been suspended after it emerged he asked technicians to break a corpse's neck, to cover up a mistake he'd made on a PM report. Also in London, at Westminster Mortuary, technicians kept stolen turkeys in the fridge (to be sold down the local pub), while at Edgware the manager smuggled illegal pornographic magazines inside coffins. Nottingham's mortuary manager sold organs and stole clothes. Even the churchyards weren't immune to the lure of crime with two Welsh gravediggers caught smashing coffins to rob the dead in Merthyr, while two teenagers on work experience in Lichfield graveyard sold bones to universities. A priest in Tywyn had developed the extraordinary habit of castrating all male bodies prior to their funerals. Coventry cold store was burgled, widely suspected to be an inside job. Twelve corpses had been pulled from fridges and ransacked (three of them ended up on the floor). In Battersea, the body of the famous TV comedian and actor Dick Emery had been left in a rat-infested garage. The list went on. Meanwhile, coroner's officers all over South London were being suspended. In Southwark, David, the 'secret' drinker decided that now was a good time to retire on health grounds, while Ted and Frank were facing trial for corruption. In total, eight London-based coroner's officers from Croydon, Battersea, Westminster and Southwark were all facing charges of corruption. Of the 43 officers that had been placed under investigation, in what was then a bit of a tradition in the police, many escaped prosecution by simply agreeing to resign, while others were moved to other duties. In the end, only six police officers were successfully prosecuted, sacked and fined. CIB2 weren't happy. The bosses down the Yard still wouldn't let them pursue leads in North London; the scandal was just too big and they wanted it gone.

I was down the pub, discussing these cases with my one friend in the coroner's office, Brian. At the end of the evening, he mentioned that he was suffering from chest pains and joked he'd be on my slab in the morning.

He died of a heart attack that night.

SOUTHWARK WAS HUGELY understaffed and morale was lower than a well-digger's shovel. I didn't think it could have sunk any lower but I soon found out there was still some way to go.

Southwark Council instructed me to compose a questionnaire on mortuary services for distribution to every council in England and Wales. The idea, so I thought, was to collect information that would help set up a national body and a national standard for the UK's mortuaries. I asked how many staff they had, how many fridge spaces, whether they operated an out-of-hours service, etc. I sent the completed questionnaire off to head office where, unbeknownst to me, they added another question: 'Do your staff receive payments from pathologists and undertakers?'

The first thing I knew about the added question was when I was at home and about to sit down to dinner. A violent knocking brought me to the front door.

It was Trevor, a superintendent at another London mortuary. 'What the hell have you done now, Everett!?' he yelled.

'What on earth are you talking about?' I replied in all innocence, reluctant to let this normally placid man into my house.

'A bloody can of worms! Thanks to you, the council's stopped all payments from the funeral directors and pathologists. That's a quarter of my salary lost, thanks to you!'

'But I don't understand,' I said, 'that's got nothing to do with me, if the council decide—'

'So this survey that's in your name, that wasn't you, was it?'

After trying and failing to calm Trevor down, I checked the following day and saw the additional question that the council had added.

'Oh Christ!'

Indeed, I soon felt as though I was on the verge of being crucified.

What few friends I had in the service soon departed once they realised that I was responsible (however misguided this understanding was) for cutting a quarter of their wages. I received death threats, and rumours were spread about my own honesty.

The real body blow arrived a few weeks later with a visit from a tax inspector. The Inland Revenue had decided to investigate every mortuary in the country and we were all assessed on extramural payments earned from the date of our appointments. Hundreds of technicians were affected, and all had to find thousands of pounds in back tax.

I was no longer welcome in the Mortuary Guild and so I resigned. I had no friends or colleagues I could call on for support. Up until this point the service had been a community, a family; we all came together in times of crisis and shared our facilities and knowledge. Now, because I had had a thief arrested and exposed corruption, I had lost everything. The obvious solution was to resign my position too; but I simply could not imagine leaving the mortuary. To work there had been my life's ambition and now I was superintendent, I lived it 24 hours a day – it was my life, to leave it would be to die. I decided I would stay in office and if I had to operate in isolation, then so be it.

I did at least have one friend in Sally, the young assistant who'd bravely come forward as a witness to George's corrupt behaviour. And, as I needed to replace George and Eric as soon as possible, I decided to hunt down my old friend and assistant from St Mary's, Pat. I found him working in a nursing home. I explained the mess I was in and what he'd be getting into, but to my delight Pat took it in his stride. The stories of corruption didn't faze him at all. We'd both seen comparatively minor levels of theft at St Mary's. The mortuary manager who came before me there had been fired for stealing from a body while one of my assistants had been accused of taking a patient's watch. A lack of evidence meant the case was never proved and so she was moved to patient records.

'I could do with a bit of excitement!' Pat exclaimed, and he arrived at Southwark the following week. So with Sally and Pat behind me, I was going do my damnedest to turn Southwark Mortuary around.

9

Questions remain

July 1984

I removed my ID card as the cab pulled up outside the Old Bailey and, walking quickly past the gaggle of TV and newspaper journalists sweltering under a blazing sun, I stepped through the front doors. After passing through security, I walked down two narrow corridors and entered Court Number One.

Like Southwark Mortuary, the facilities at the Old Bailey were in desperate need of updating; the courtrooms were cramped and stuffy and, since the onset of a heatwave, trials had become feats of endurance, especially for the bewigged QCs and judges.

I found a seat behind the witness stand, which gave me a good view of the accused and the public gallery. Counsels took their places, acting as though this was just another day at court, but it would have been impossible to ignore the three sets of families above in the public gallery, looking down upon them. The parents of the murdered and the accused were sat just a few metres from one another. This was their long-awaited day of justice, the two sides full of hope – one for acquittal, the others for a life sentence. Tension was running high and the journalists who filled the tiny press box, along with every free gallery space they'd been able to find, could hardly keep still. Memories of the case were fresh in people's minds, as were the front-page photographs of the victims' funerals, which, overwhelmed with flowers, had brought South London to a standstill: 'London's Romeo and Juliet' was the *Standard*'s headline, a dramatic if inaccurate comparison, accompanied by an unforgettable picture of the horse-drawn hearses covered in flowers and a procession of mourners as far as the eye could see, all the way down Borough High Street.

Finally, order was called, the court fell silent and we stood for the judge. I wasn't here to give evidence or to provide witness testimony, but I had been involved in this case from day one, and I wanted to see it through to the end.

THE STORY BEGAN on a snowy Sunday morning the previous February, the month after George's sentencing. Although things were far from perfect at the mortuary (our facilities were still hopelessly outdated and we were constantly short-staffed), Southwark was now shipshape, and had remained free of criminal and bureaucratic incident since his conviction. With Pat's help, we had managed to stay on top of the administrative side which meant, with a bit of luck, about one in four Sundays could be devoted entirely to leisure.

I was at home enjoying a pipe while trying unsuccessfully to crack a few clues on *The Sunday Times* crossword when the phone rang. I glared at it, then reached for the receiver.

'Sorry to get you out on a day like this,' Professor Mant said, 'but there's a double murder in Mint Street. A car's on its way to pick you up.'

Mint Street, it turned out, was just a five-minute stroll from my apartment, but I was glad to have been spared the walk. As soon as I was out of the squad car, a woodentop leaned forward and spoke quietly into my ear.

'Be careful, sir, won't you?'

He pointed skywards and, wondering what on earth he could be referring to, I looked up. There was a fire station tower and on top of it was a TV camera crew. How they had managed this in the early hours of Sunday morning remains a mystery. I followed the direction their camera was pointing in and spotted a large yellow dumper truck at the end of the street in a small car park next to a playing field.

I was greeted by DI Dougie Campbell.

'Morning Peter,' he said, shaking my hand. 'Tricky scene. I'm afraid Professor Mant's still struggling in from Surrey.'

Dougie filled me in as we approached the dumper truck, where a lab liaison officer was struggling to preserve the evidence under a tarpaulin. The snow had turned to hail.

'Local lady, Doreen Gavaghan, found the bodies, or rather her dog did. It wouldn't stop barking at the truck so she climbed up and took a peek over the side.'

As the lab liaison officer shifted the tarpaulin it almost blew away in the wind, which was when a photojournalist snapped the picture that would be on the front pages of most of the newspapers the following day: myself and Dougie, peering into the digger's bucket, studying two partially-exposed bodies folded awkwardly into the bottom. I just had time to see the faces of a boy and a girl, both teenagers, both partially undressed and covered in quite a bit of blood, when Professor Mant arrived.

'We'll need to climb into the digger,' I said. 'Are you able?'

The prof shook his head and reached instinctively for his back. 'Not without a ladder.'

Constables were sent to fetch ladders and more tarpaulins. Soon, we just about had a private, sheltered place in which to work and, with a little help, Professor Mant and I were in the bucket with the bodies, woollen gloves swapped for rubber ones.

Professor Mant knelt down and looked closely at the boy's throat. 'Knife wound. Most likely severed the carotid,' he said, as I took Polaroids and made notes. I could see a ligature around the girl's neck. Her tongue was protruding slightly and her throat and face were heavily bruised. She was naked below the waist. The boy's trousers had been pulled down and his penis was exposed.

'Any idea of how long they've been dead?' Dougie asked from the outside, peering over the side of the bucket.

'About twelve hours is my best guess,' Professor Mant replied.

At this point the hail turned to torrential rain and we decided to abort any further examination at the scene and to get the bodies to the mortuary as soon as possible, to prevent trace evidence from being washed away. With hindsight, I should have ordered the entire digger to be brought along. The mortuary had a large yard in which it could have been stored for further examination, but as it was, we carefully unloaded the bodies, placed them in plastic body bags, sealed them tightly with Sellotape, and I rode with them in the van to Southwark.

Once we were in the mortuary's reception room, I cut open the bags with a large pair of scissors and, helped by Dougie along with his sergeant, a quiet, serious-looking man in his late twenties, we lifted the bodies onto a white square on the floor where the police photographer took pictures of them from all angles, front and back, getting close-ups of any wounds.

We then went through their pockets. Neither of them had any identification. We undressed the bodies and bagged the clothes before taking swabs. As the photographer took more pictures, Cliff sealed the body bags inside new bags. These would be forensically examined at the lab, just in case any trace evidence, such as a perpetrator's hair, blood or a broken nail, was inside.

Once the bodies were on the table, Professor Mant started with the boy.

'An eleven-centimetre-long oblique incised wound of the neck. The epiglottis is severed, as is the left carotid artery.'

He then took a probe and slid it carefully into the entry wound until it stopped and took a measurement of the depth, which, in this case, was eight centimetres. Being careful not to cut into the wound in the boy's throat, Professor Mant cut the Y-incision from the neck to the pubis and quickly removed the organs.

'Blood is present in the oesophagus and has been inhaled into the lungs,' Professor Mant concluded. 'Death was instantaneous.'

Photographs were then taken of the wound's interior before the prof carefully checked the cranium for bruising and then removed the brain. More swabs were taken, along with samples of blood and urine and, that done, the organs were placed into black plastic bags, which were in turn placed back into the body, which was sewn up, then placed in the fridge, ready for the funeral director.

The same procedure followed for the girl.

Bruising covered her neck and lower face, and her tongue protruded, a common sign of strangulation.

'There are petechial haemorrhages above the ligature mark,' Professor Mant said before looking into the girl's mouth.

'Hang on, that's odd.'

Dougie stepped forward as Professor Mant reached in with a pair of tweezers and extracted a small roll of brown paper. There was no writing on it and the item was placed in an evidence bag. This turned out to be a piece of rubbish that had most likely blown into her open mouth while she was still in the digger's bucket.

'Injuries to the sides of the lower jaw and back of the head are consistent with the deceased having been firmly gripped and having her head struck against a firm surface. Cause of death is compression of the neck.'

'Any sign that she was sexually assaulted?' Dougie asked.

Professor Mant shook his head.

WHILE I BROUGHT Professor Mant up to my flat for a bite to eat, Dougie ventured back out into what was now total darkness. The snow, hail and now rain had served to remove all trace, if there had ever been any, of how the bodies had been transported to the digger but a missing persons report had been filed and the descriptions matched the victims perfectly.

Robert Vaughan and Michelle Sadler, both seventeen and going steady for eighteen months, had just become engaged. They'd failed to show for a family party the previous evening and their parents had called the police. Checking their place of work, a small factory a few streets from where the bodies had been found, detectives found pools of blood in the loading bay and in the toilets. From this, they concluded that Robert had been attacked from behind while he was at the urinal, which explained why his penis had been exposed. Chillingly, in both the loading bay and the toilets, they found the killer's bloody footprints.

Robert and Michelle had been working overtime, on their own, on Saturday night; they were trying to save money for their wedding. Interviews with their colleagues revealed a possible suspect: David Carty, eighteen, a relatively new employee. Carty had apparently been making unwanted advances towards Michelle for some days.

As soon as Dougie saw Carty, he knew he had his man: Carty, who was slender and about five-foot-eight, was nervous and constantly fidgeting.

At first Carty claimed he'd spent the day in Oxford Street, shopping, but confronted with the fact that detectives had found blood on a pair of trainers in his bedroom, and that these trainers matched the bloody footprints at the scene, he admitted that he'd stopped by the factory looking for Robert and Michelle (claiming they were good friends) and found the bodies. Getting blood on his shoes, he realised that the police would blame him (especially because he was black, he argued), and so he'd hidden the bodies, using a wheelbarrow from work to wheel them through the snowy streets of London for almost a kilometre, until he came across the dumper truck. Why he failed to properly clean up the scene of the murder and to throw away his trainers, Carty wasn't able to explain. 'I don't know what I was thinking,' was all he could tell Dougie.

Meanwhile, the lab, having analysed blood found on Michelle's body reported that it was B+. Only 5 per cent of people are B+. Dougie thought the case was all sewn up when Carty turned out to be a match but then the lab called back: Robert's blood was also B+!

Although the evidence pointing to Carty's guilt was strong, it was circumstantial. The Crown Prosecution Service (CPS) was nervous about going ahead with a murder charge based solely on circumstantial evidence after having suffered a pair of high-profile losses at the Old Bailey in recent weeks. One of the acquitted had been black and a small riot had broken out in Brixton afterwards. The 1981 Brixton riots were still fresh in everyone's memory, and so, understandably, the police did not want to increase racial tensions by arresting a black man from the Brixton area for the murders of two white people without solid proof. Then there was the fact that there were plenty of clever barristers who were experts in crushing circumstantial evidence and establishing reasonable doubt in the minds of a jury.

Then Dougie had a bright idea.

A few weeks earlier, a police officer had been on patrol in Kilburn, north-west London, and noted an illegally parked car on the high street. He'd jotted down the number plate with a biro on his hand, thinking to have it towed, but other more urgent crimes soon took over and he forgot all about it until the next day when he learned that the same make and model of that car had been used in a bank robbery on Kilburn High Road. Of course, he'd washed his hands by now. He told his sergeant, who told the DI, who told the commander, who'd heard of a new laser technology being trialled at the police lab in Lambeth. The constable was sent down to the lab where scientists fired a laser at his hand, revealing the microscopic traces of ink that hadn't been washed out and presto, the number plate appeared. The car was traced and the robbers caught.

What, Dougie wondered, if this worked for fingerprints? Perhaps this laser could highlight enough microscopic traces of dirt to reveal an impression, meaning they could be lifted from the skin of Michelle's throat. It was late when I got the call; I was just getting ready for bed but a few minutes later I was in the back of the mortuary van with Michelle's body, bound for the lab in Pratt Walk, just behind Lambeth Palace. There was one significant problem. When I arrived, the lab technicians informed me that they didn't have a suitable trolley on which to transport the body to the laser room and I, assuming they would have, hadn't thought to bring one.

By now word had got out about our experiment and police commanders from all over London were on their way to observe. The pressure was on. When the lab technicians turned up at our van with a tea trolley pinched from the staff canteen, I baulked at the idea, but only for a minute or so. I felt terrible, but I thought if it meant we might catch the murderer and prevent a race riot, it had to be done. So, after struggling with Michelle's bagged up body in an alleyway behind the police lab, we laid it carefully on the trolley. After a few metres the trolley started to collapse, but we were too far from the van to carry the body back.

'Just keep going!' I puffed at the white-faced lab officers who weren't used to transporting bodies at the best of times, let alone in a dark alleyway in the middle of the night. The lab also happened to share space with a holding house for prisoners who were due to appear in London courts the following day, and our next problem turned out to be the dozen or so badly parked prison vans that blocked our way. We were forced to take a ridiculously complex route right below the walls of Lambeth Palace; the Archbishop of Canterbury would have got the shock of his life if he'd happened to glance out of one of the many windows just then.

We scrambled through the building, just about squeezing into the lift and, breathless, flushed and panting, we got poor Michelle's body onto the table in the laser lab before twelve impatient police commanders, all in uniform, all wearing protective sunglasses: a surreal sight to say the least. We all craned forward as the laser shone on Michelle's neck, all of us willing the prints to appear like a photo in the developing tray. Gradually, as the first signs of faded outlines appeared, there was a collective gasp of excitement. A minute later, however, they remained just that. We could find nothing definitive. The killer must have had clean hands, and our primitive technology was not up to the job. We left despondent, and once Michelle's body was safely back in the van, the lab staff returned the now broken tea trolley. The canteen staff would never know the macabre circumstances that had led to its ruin.

THE JUDGE'S DIRECTIONS given, the jury had retired and I met with Dougie in the cafeteria.

'It'll be fine,' I said. 'There's no way Carty's walking out of here a free man.'

Dougie nodded, uncertain.

'I think so too but you can never predict a jury,' he said quietly. 'And there's a lot riding on this case, London's fragile peace for a start, never mind my career.'

The canteen was crowded and I spotted Helena Kennedy, Carty's defence barrister, looking for somewhere to sit. Dougie turned to follow my gaze and waved her over.

Even though, technically speaking, they were on opposite sides, there was rarely any animosity between barristers and police because we all subscribed to the justice system and were therefore bound by the rules of the game. Everyone simply did the best they could with the information they had and hoped they'd done enough.

'So how was it for you?' Dougie asked as Helena took her seat.

'Impossible to tell,' she said. 'When the courtroom's spotlight is on you, you can't tell how the jury are taking it. They often surprise me.'

And with that, the jury surprised us. The general increase of hubbub and movement in the room told us that they had announced the completion of their deliberations. It had taken them less than 30 minutes. Leaving our drinks on the table, we hurried back and I took my seat with its view of the accused and the public gallery. I studied Carty's face as the foreman stood up and answered the judge's standard questions before coming to the crunch. 'And will you now tell the court your verdict?'

'Guilty.'

The briefest of flickers passed over Carty's face, a slight tremble and then nothing. Cries and shouts came from the public gallery. Carty's family had been confident of a not-guilty verdict while Robert and Michelle's families had collapsed in relief that at last this terrible ordeal was over. Once the clerk called for silence, the judge announced that there was no need to delay sentencing. The guilty verdict called for one sentence only and that was life. As journalists stampeded for the exit, I caught Helena's eye. She gave a little shrug, which I took to mean: 'You win some, you lose some.'

Carty still displayed no reaction, only glancing at the judge as he was led down the steps to the holding cells. A good friend of mine, a high-ranking prison officer, had once told me how, back in the days of execution, after the guilty had been sentenced to death, they'd usually remain silent for a while, but: 'By the time they were back in their cell they were practically cheerful,' he said. 'Full of jokes. I don't know if it was shock, or a release of tension after having to wait for the verdict for a long time. It was only when their final appeal failed that their will broke. Then they had nothing to say at all.'

I caught up with Dougie in the reception area and shook his hand. He was already with the families and, amid the crowd and the hubbub, he introduced me to Robert's mother. 'And what do you do?' she asked. 'Were you involved in my son's case?'

Not wanting to upset her, I explained I worked on the technical side of evidence gathering and she nodded, thanked me, and I saw in her eyes the strain these events had put on her. It was terrible enough to lose your son, but to know that he had been murdered and then have to endure a trial – I couldn't imagine the suffering she must have gone through, let alone the strength required to experience such an ordeal. And it wasn't quite over yet: TV crews, curious onlookers and courtroom staff thronged on the pavement.

'Can't you sneak them out the back?' I asked Dougie.

'I'm sorry; we're not allowed to,' he replied.

So the families walked out into the afternoon heat, to be dazzled by the sun and then suffocated by the reporters that gathered around as they climbed into cabs. A minute later, I caught a cab of my own, and as I travelled back to Southwark I puzzled over a question which would never be solved, not unless Carty one day decided to confess: how had he managed to carry both bodies from the murder scene, for almost a kilometre over icy streets and lift them up, practically to head height, and into the truck? Carty was short and of slight build, and Robert and Michelle were healthy seventeen year olds, weighing about 80 and 65 kilos respectively. Carty said he had used a wheelbarrow, and I knew I would struggle to wheel 50 kilograms more than 100 metres in a straight line on a dry day. Had there been an accomplice who'd helped Carty dispose of the bodies? Always in such cases, questions remain that must go unanswered.

10

Disaster in the sky

June 1985

It was Saturday 24 June 1985 and the memories of the corruption scandal had at last started to fade. I was enjoying the late afternoon sun and the calming sights and sounds of a county cricket match at Kent's home ground, pipe in one hand, cool bitter in the other. Thanks to Pat, my ever-reliable deputy and general bulwark against chaos, I'd managed to book some much-needed time off. The final over had just begun when the peace was interrupted by the extremely loud shriek of my emergency pager, causing me to spill my bitter as I rushed to retrieve the damn thing from my pocket. Amid angry stares I hurried away to find a telephone.

Expecting to be called to a murder, I was more than a little surprised to learn that I was booked on a flight to Cork in two hours' time. A major air disaster: Air India Flight 182, carrying 307 passengers and 22 crew from

Montreal to Delhi had vanished from the radar somewhere over the Irish Sea.

I'd joined the British Air Crash Repatriation and Home Office Major Disaster teams while I was still at St Mary's, but this was the first time my services had been called upon. It was run independently of my employer, so any assistance I gave had to come out of my annual leave, but fortunately my time was paid for by Kenyon, a well-known firm of London funeral directors who'd established themselves as the world's only true experts in the field of mass fatality incidents.

Kenyon had been at the forefront of major disaster management in the UK since 1906, when Harold and Herbert Kenyon, the sons of James Kenyon, creator of the JH Kenyon funeral business, were called to the site of a train which had derailed at high speed near Salisbury railway station, on 1 July 1906. Twenty-eight people were killed, many of them wealthy New Yorkers travelling from the port of Plymouth to London. Just over two weeks later, Herbert Kenyon accompanied five of the deceased back to New York on the Cunard steam ship *Campania*. Their international work began in 1930, after the world's largest airship, the R101, crashed on its inaugural flight in Beavous in France, killing all but five of its 54 VIP passengers and crew. Among the dead was the British Secretary of State for Air, Lord Thomson of Cardington, a champion of the airship. HM Government asked Kenyon to travel to France to repatriate the bodies of the British victims. From that day forth, they were the first people the government called in the wake of a mass fatality incident. Members of the team came from all over the United

Kingdom and included embalmers, pathologists and technicians; all of whom were on standby to fly anywhere in the world with only two hours' notice.

A communications headquarters was opened in Marylebone while vanloads of equipment was rushed to Cork. Other members of the repatriation team had already departed for Canada and India to act as family liaison officers (FLOs). By the time I was over the Irish Sea, it had been declared a non-survivor crash. Like the rest of the repatriation team, I travelled incognito. I was booked onto the flight as a travelling salesman (in those days, passengers flying to Southern Ireland had to complete a security vetting form stating the reason for their journey). We were also asked to take other precautions, the most peculiar of which was to write our name and date of birth on a piece of wax paper and clamp it in our mouth, so our identity could be quickly be ascertained in the event *we* were caught up in a disaster.

The sun was low as we approached Cork, and the sea gleamed while the bright green land threw long shadows out to the west. A bright white island lighthouse completed a picture-perfect and peaceful scene. Although by now I considered myself immune to the effects of dead bodies that so troubled other people, I started to wonder how I was going to cope with fatalities on such a grand scale.

After being met at the airport by two police officers, I was driven to a remote part of the airfield where army helicopters were landing, delivering the bodies, all in military green body bags, to army vehicles. Seeing the number of bags, it was almost overwhelming. At Southwark on a busy day, I might see twenty bodies. Here, there were dozens upon dozens.

We drove to Jury's Hotel through empty streets. News of the disaster had by now spread throughout the town, and its inhabitants stayed indoors out of respect. Upon arrival at the hotel I was delighted to run into Des Henley, a good friend who'd also devoted his life to death. Des was considered the father of the mortuary team, with many years' disaster experience. He also held the unusual regal title of 'The Royal Embalmer' and had embalmed the bodies of King George VI at Sandringham House in 1952, Queen Mary at Marlborough House in 1953, and Sir Winston Churchill in his London home at 28 Hyde Park Gate in 1965. Des, a tall, quiet man, was exceptionally modest, but his great deeds would not go unnoticed. A few years later he was made an OBE for his services to disaster management.

I also bumped into Bernie Simms, head of odontology, who would help identify the victims through dental records. It was hard not to bump into Bernie, a 150-kilo giant of a man. I once saw a photo of him while in Thailand, posing next to a giant stone statue of Buddha. They looked so alike that you couldn't tell the difference. Despite his size, Bernie was light on his feet and worked tirelessly, with true passion.

The situation was quite surreal; although the town was quiet, tourists, no doubt in holiday mood and not having seen the news, were in full party mode. Our team of twenty of death's servants dined in comparative silence until we were joined late in the evening by senior members of the Irish Cabinet, including Bertie Ahern, the future Irish prime minister, along with Christopher Kenyon, Kenyon's CEO, a charming man who fascinated the politicians with tales from his remarkable career. Also present to liven our mood was Professor John Harbison (known to all as Jack), the state pathologist for Eire, whose untidy white hair made him look older than he was but whose eyes sparkled with wit and intelligence. He joked about how it had been 25 years since he last had a live patient and explained that he became interested in pathology after he discovered he was a 'medical misfit', who just wasn't interested in sick people.

Woken shortly after dawn, I stumbled out of bed and into a glorious sunrise. I admired it with a degree of trepidation. This was going to be one hell of a job. Relatives across three continents were waiting for closure. We had hundreds of victims to identify. The sooner we could ID the bodies, the better it was for the victims' relatives. In my experience, families faced with tragedy grasp at straws and go into immediate denial. Maybe their relative missed the flight; maybe she was transferred to another plane; maybe they got the wrong flight number; maybe she survived. Such hope is futile, but until they have incontrovertible proof of death, that hope can drive them to the point of insanity.

A temporary mortuary was established at Cork County Hospital. The patients' social hut was commandeered for use as the post-mortem room, with the staff room designated as mortuary control.

As the first bodies were brought into the hut, telephone engineers set up fax and phone links to Toronto, London and Mumbai, and a notice board was cleared for photos of the victims that would be faxed to us by the family liaison teams, to aid us with identification.

I was appointed reception officer and turned my attention to the dozens of green body bags. The process of identification was, in some ways, very simple, but at the same time, incredibly challenging. In the case of any disaster, asking relatives and loved ones to view victims is simply not acceptable. Sudden bereavement is near impossible to come to terms with in the immediate aftermath, and there have been cases of non-recognition, as the bereaved so desperately want it to not be their loved one who has died. For these reasons, the identification process becomes even more important. In essence, for each and every body and body part of a victim involved in a mass fatality disaster, we have to satisfy the coroner via matching ante-mortem data (things that are known about the deceased pre death – information from friends, work colleagues and families, for example) and post-mortem data, as to why we believe body or body part number 'x' belongs to person 'y'. The police do not have the power to confirm identity, only the coroner can do this based on the evidence presented.

DNA testing was still more than a decade away, so the accepted scientific criteria were odontology (dentistry) and fingerprints, with confirmation of identity via personal effects. Also, 'mechanical fit' would be used for the body parts that would arrive in their own separate body bags. If the parts could be 'pieced together' precisely enough to prove that they belonged to the same person, then this could also be submitted as supporting evidence.

As well as looking for clues as to the identity of each victim, we had to determine as far as possible whether anything about their bodies could tell us how the plane had crashed. As the investigation into the cause was proceeding with great speed, we were keen to examine the pilots first to establish whether something like a heart attack or seizure could have caused the crash, or if any pilot had been drinking or taking drugs, for example.

I took a deep breath and started to pull the zip. I had long conditioned myself to not see whatever was in the bag as a person. What was there was merely a vehicle, a shell that had taken the person through life. It was then that I realised that, although I might be conditioned to death through my daily work, my police assistants were probably not so accustomed. I glanced up and I saw fear on their faces. These poor buggers were here simply because they happened to be on duty that day. Despite their professionalism and willingness to do what was asked, they just weren't prepared.

I cleared my throat and started talking. A bit of conversation might keep their minds occupied, I thought, and help to suppress any fits of fainting. I chatted about how I saw the body as a vehicle and then started to talk about the process, what they were going to be doing and more importantly why.

I unzipped the bag and then stopped in surprise. The body, of a middle-aged woman wrapped in an orange blanket, was intact and there was no blood, but what had surprised me was the fact that she was naked. I quickly checked a couple of other body bags. Also naked. I rushed off and found Jack.

'The victims are all naked. Where are their clothes?'

A quick investigation revealed that the body recovery team had undressed the victims on the ship before placing them in the body bags, thinking that they were helping us. This had the opposite effect, as clothes would have provided key pieces of evidence in terms of identification. They might have passports and tickets in their pockets, for example, or a distinctive item of clothing that would help the family liaison team identify them from family photo albums.

'Too late for us to do anything about it now,' Jack said, and so we cracked on.

As we began to work, I saw the tension in the police officers dissipating. It's odd, having one's sensory expectations confounded; the lack of blood and the fact there was no particular smell of death, I think, helped. The reality was less horrific than imagined. I was confident that if the cops could cope with this they could cope with the next couple of days and get through it all okay.

Together we filled in reception forms, which recorded every single detail about the person that we could find; eye colour, scars, skin blemishes, birthmarks, tattoos, hair length/type, height and build. Many of the Indian victims of the crash were wearing lots of jewellery which hadn't been removed by the body recovery team: bangles, rings and necklaces. This would provide us with an excellent basis from which to start identifying each body.

From reception the body went to Bernie, who recorded each victim's teeth chart. Most people have dental treatment during their life and the more treatment they have, the more unique they are likely to be. Even fillings are done differently and so can be distinctive on their own. Bernie's team carefully logged evidence of any dental treatment and, as long as the ante-mortem dental records were up to date, these could be matched and identification confirmed, usually very quickly and with 100 per cent accuracy.

FLOs were gathering dental records of those listed on the flight manifest. They were also visiting the home addresses of the deceased victims and, in extremely difficult circumstances, were trying to lift latent fingerprints from surfaces and items used by the deceased. Most people do not have an official fingerprint record unless they have been a suspect in or convicted of a crime; so, in terms of evidence for the coroner in these circumstances, latent prints are crucial. There are, of course, moral issues when considering the use of official fingerprints such as convictions records, as details are likely to be made public in court.

While we were dealing with the dead, the FLOs had the delicate task of interviewing grieving relatives and friends to obtain personal details about clothing worn that day, any marks, scars, tattoos the victims had and any personal items they may have been carrying. All of these elements formed the ante-mortem data, and all details, just as with those obtained in the mortuary, were meticulously logged.

It is worth stressing that the collection of ante-mortem and post-mortem data happens simultaneously, so those working within the mortuary do not usually see what has been harvested on the ante-mortem side and vice-versa, which means that neither can influence the other and each remains impartial and objective.

After Bernie had completed his examination, the body was moved to the fingerprint station. A team of four pathologists carried out the post-mortems under Jack's supervision. With the post-mortems complete, the victims then went to the embalmers prior to lying in a tented chapel of rest.

I slipped into automatic mode as we processed the next body, and the next. The pace was rapid but steady. By the early afternoon I was pleased with how everything was going and how the police officers were coping. As each bag was placed on the table, we declared ourselves ready, and I unzipped it. Another, lighter bag had arrived and so I braced myself to expect an incomplete body. When I unzipped it, however, I froze. The body, of a child, was in perfect condition. A boy, about ten years old. I glanced at the police officers and saw the shock registering on their faces. The child's eyes were wide open. The sight even took my breath away. His whole life had been in front of him and now here he was, four stunned men looking down upon him, trying their best to cope with the impossibly difficult task they were now facing. We lifted the boy out of the bag and removed the blanket. Exceptionally, he was still wearing an item of clothing – a T-shirt with a fantastic picture of a green dinosaur that I am sure would have been the envy of all of his friends.

THE NEXT DAY went as the first, with our preparations now feeling ritualistic. It took us six days to complete the examinations of 181 recovered bodies. Each evening, Bernie, Jack, Des and I would retire to the hotel bar and, after conducting our own PM of the day's events, would try to take our minds to happier places by swapping tall tales over Irish whiskey.

By the sixth day, I had a massive sense of satisfaction. I knew without doubt that we had recorded each and every body and body part correctly, and was confident the bereaved could now be assured that their loved one would be returned to them for final closure.

I was passing by the noticeboard, which by now was full of photos of missing loved ones, when one picture brought me to a halt. It was of a little boy wearing a T-shirt with a bright green dinosaur in it. I took the photo to the identification team who compared it with the boy's PM photo. 'It's not him,' I was told.

'What? But that T-shirt? Surely they match.'

'The dinosaur's facing the wrong way. It must be another version of the same image.'

Disappointed, I left them to carry on with their important work and it was only weeks later, after telling a police photographer about this incident that he told me that, depending on how you process an image, it can be flipped so that it mirrors reality, so that had definitely been the right child.

WE WERE JUST about to pack up and fly back to London when one of the embalmers, having trouble removing fluids, made a discovery. A piece of metal embedded in a victim's leg. This was shrapnel.

A fragment from an explosion.

Up until this point, the disaster had been treated as a

standard crash; now it was multiple murder. The bodies all had to be re-examined and shrapnel was found in some more victims, those who'd been sitting closest to the bomb that had caused the plane to crash. The incident was designated an act of terrorism, and we were joined by representatives of the Royal Canadian Mounted Police and various intelligence agencies from the UK, India and the USA.

Once our job was finally completed, our conclusions, along with ante-mortem data, were sent to the reconciliation unit, which was made up of another set of police officers and other professionals such as fingerprint experts, dentists and forensic scientists who work independently of the on-site teams to match ante-mortem with post-mortem data. When a match has been established, the evidence is presented to the identification commission. The identification commission considered the evidence as to why body or body part number 'x' is thought to belong to that of person 'y'. If enough information and evidence based on the criteria set has been submitted, then Her Majesty's Coroner will formerly declare the person as deceased and will open and adjourn the inquest. If HM Coroner is not satisfied with the evidence gathered on either the ante- or post-mortem side, then the police are required to obtain further evidence and re-present the case. In this case, the body of every recovered victim – even the ten-year-old boy – was correctly identified and returned to their families.

Working on an emergency response team is very rewarding. You never know where you will be tomorrow; you could be in Japan working on an air crash or in Australia dealing with a mass murder. However, the duties are grim and attract much stress and long separation from loved ones back home. In the cases of the Lockerbie and the Herald of Free Enterprise disasters, the teams were away for Christmas. Beyond all doubt, this group of professional, caring, unsung heroes deserve praise, and we should be proud of them because they have to deal with incredibly difficult sights that once seen can never be forgotten.

In my case, the incident in Cork that really caught me by surprise came when I was taking a short pipe break. Large marquees had been erected in the hospital grounds; these acted as chapels of rest and were supervised by nuns. Following embalming, the bodies were dressed in white shrouds and laid out in neat rows; each victim had a red rose placed on his or her chest. One marquee had been designated as the children's tent: 60 bodies aged between six months and fifteen years of age lay neatly side by side. As Ian Hill, a Home Office pathologist known to all as Biggles (he was a former RAF Wing Commander), said to me: 'This is the photo that should be in the papers to show the world what terrorism achieves.'

As most of us were parents we found it very difficult to enter this tent. As I strolled under blue summer skies puffing on my pipe, I was brought to a halt by the sight of a group of nuns carrying a six-foot teddy bear into the tent. This beautiful gesture was meant well, but it did more harm than good for those working to recover and identify the bodies – it rammed home only too hard the cruel loss of these innocent souls.

11

Life goes on

September 1985

Rudely awoken by the shrill ringing of the telephone, I snapped out my arm and fumbled for the receiver as Wendy, who now worked at the other end of life's spectrum – as a midwife – groaned in exasperation. The bedside phone always seemed to ring a few hours after she returned from one of her marathon shifts. I fumbled with the receiver, holding it the wrong way up, but even at a distance I could clearly hear the booming voice of Professor Johnson: 'Morning Everett, it's the prof. I'm in the PM room with a very nasty case. Get down here ASAP!'

I struggled out of bed and into my suit and staggered out into what was a beautiful September dawn. As I strode along the narrow path that ran from my flat to the park behind the mortuary, I was surprised to see several dog handlers, their hounds' noses to the soil in ferocious concentration. Police cars were parked outside and several uniformed and plain-clothed officers were in the yard. To my great surprise, a dog handler was in the PM room with his mutt.

'Get that thing out of here!' I exclaimed to the startled handler. 'What the hell do you think you're doing in here with that creature?'

The officer apologised and hurried out.

Professor Johnson was already there, pacing up and down, having – unusually for him – ignored the dog. Only the room's sidelights were on, leaving the table shrouded in shadows, but I could see enough to tell me that the body of a child was lying upon it. The prof stopped pacing when he saw me and snapped: 'It's not him!'

I switched on the overhead light and saw the body was of a girl, about five years old, wearing a yellow dress. One of her shoes was missing. We'd been expecting to receive a call about six-year-old Barry Lewis, who'd vanished while playing near his home in Walworth some days earlier.

'This is Stacey Kavanagh, four years old,' Professor Johnson continued. 'Police found her in Southwark Park after she was reported abducted from the communal gardens at their block of flats. A neighbour found one of her shoes there.'

'Where's the murder squad?' I asked, starting to prep the room.

'Still at the scene. Another little girl's missing: Stacey's friend, Tina Beechook. She's seven.'

Pat arrived moments later and, immediately reading the situation, joined us in silent preparation. It was a genuine relief to me to have Pat by my side for, in the two years since starting at Southwark, this mild-mannered, unflappable Irishman had proven himself to be utterly reliable. Freshly-promoted Detective Chief Inspector (DCI) Dougie Campbell arrived shortly after, along with two detectives, the police photographer and Cliff Smith the lab liaison officer. We nodded our hellos; the scene was far too sad for a 'good morning', and we worked quietly, just speaking when necessary, to give the details for the PM record. Despite our grim task, it was comforting to be among professionals, all doing a very difficult job, the importance of which united us all in a common cause. Nothing would be missed, no stone would go unturned in the search for justice, to bring some sense of closure to Stacey's parents who were no doubt extremely distressed, having to face the day that every parent dreads.

There were no defence injuries, a sign that perhaps Stacey had known her killer. She hadn't been sexually abused, something we'd all suspected given the number of child abductions that had taken place in recent months. Not only was Barry Lewis missing, the sexually-abused body of three-year-old Leoni Keating had recently been found bound and gagged in a Suffolk canal.

In fact, the only injury to little Stacey was the one that had killed her: strangulation. 'It wasn't with bare hands,' Professor Johnson explained. 'From the markings I can tell that some kind of ligature was used. As to the type, I would suggest a cord. As to the material, I can't say. There might be hemp fibres in her clothes if someone was using rope, but that's for Mr Smith's colleagues to find out.'

As the days went on and there was no sign of Tina, the streets of Bermondsey were transformed. Children no longer played outside. Local residents formed vigilante groups, performing their own searches and patrols, questioning anyone they thought looked like a stranger, sometimes becoming quite aggressive, especially when the strangers turned out to be members of the press that had flooded into the area, desperate to get any kind of scoop. Dozens of police officers searched houses, wooded glades and the Docklands area. They became a familiar sight to the residents of the block of flats where the two girls had lived: a grey brick tenement that overlooked wasteland, beyond which were visible the cranes of the Docklands.

'At least they're united in tragedy,' Pat said later that week, thinking about the girls' families as we finished reconstituting the body of a man who'd poisoned himself. An engineer, his body had been found in his car.

Pat was right: in some sense this was a small silver lining. In recent weeks, racial tensions in the estates of Bermondsey, fuelled by allegations of police brutality and tabloid headlines about unemployment and poverty, linking them to immigration, had threatened to explode into violence. Pat and I had found ourselves at the centre of this storm when a twelve-year-old white boy had been brought into the mortuary. He'd purchased a toxic glue from a newsagent who happened to be Pakistani, sniffed it to try to get high and perished in the attempt. When certain parts of the community found out the newsagent's ethnicity, they seized upon it as an outlet for their rage. The shopkeeper had to be taken into protective custody, but a near riot took place outside Bermondsey police station with cries of awful racial epithets.

Stacey was white, but Tina's mother, Mirella, 26, was from Mauritius, an island in the Indian Ocean, and, for now at least, any racial differences were thrown aside as mothers were united by the grief, fear and sympathy that hits the community in the wake of the murder of a child, reinforced by the fact that another little girl was missing and the killer was still out there. Mirella appeared on the news, physically supported by friends and neighbours, begging for her missing daughter's safe return.

THE FOLLOWING SATURDAY, with still no sign of Barry Lewis or Tina Beechook, Wendy and I were spending the morning shopping. We'd just settled down for lunch when my pager went off. A squad car arrived minutes later, and I was whisked back to the mortuary, which was besieged by press and public alike, with more people arriving by the second. A couple of constables, on the verge of being overwhelmed, were trying to hold the growing mob back. Inside, on the mortuary table, was a large suitcase. One didn't need to be a detective to guess what was inside.

Cliff was already there, looking troubled. I asked him what was wrong. 'We tried to keep it secret, so we put the suitcase in a box and I walked with it to the van on my own. No one saw but by the time I got here, the press had somehow found out and I was snapped walking in with it. I think

I'm going to be on the front pages tomorrow.' He was quite correct, as it turned out.

Dougie's team had found out from a neighbour that Tina's mother was holding another neighbour's keys while she was away on holiday. Mirella's flat had already been searched and nothing suspicious had been found, but when police searched the neighbour's flat, they found a suitcase under the bed. Tina's body was hidden inside, along with a length of electrical cord, taken from Mirella's vacuum cleaner. Mirella and her husband, Ravi, 30, were taken into custody. As they were led away from their flat, neighbours crowded their windows and balconies, jeering racist abuse.

To Scotland Yard's great embarrassment, they belatedly discovered that six years earlier Mirella had spent time in Broadmoor, after attempting to poison her first baby. This child, Sabrina, had been taken into care.

Gradually, with the help of a Harley Street psychiatrist, Dr Raghunandan Gaind, Dougie pieced the story together. Dr Gaind's questions to Mirella revealed her to be 'vulnerable, obsessional, rigid and stubborn'. She talked about black magic and voodoo, claiming that scratches on her body had been caused by 'the evil eye' and that Ravi's ex-girlfriend had put a spell on her. Haunted by voices telling her to sacrifice the children, Mirella had taken both Tina and Stacey to Southwark Park. After sending Tina away to play, she strangled Stacey and hid her body under some leaves. She then took Tina home, stopping off on the way to buy some sweets. Tina kept asking where Stacey was, and when they arrived back at their flat Mirella Beechook strangled Tina with the electrical flex.

Mirella was charged with two counts of murder and remanded to stand trial. A devastated Ravi, who didn't know about his wife's past, and who seemed to be in genuine shock, was released, albeit under police protection, and had to move to another part of the UK for his own safety.

THE RACIAL TENSIONS in the area failed to subside, and it was exacerbated by police violence and racial profiling. Apart from abusing stop-and-search laws, targeting anyone who wasn't white, I personally heard police officers boasting about the beating they gave to suspects – they prided themselves on being equally nasty to all colours and creeds. On the side of a police van, under the official logo 'Securicor Cares,' someone had scrawled 'D-Division doesn't give a shit.' They claimed that their strategy worked. Criminals who lived in the area knew that if they didn't want to get beaten up then they should operate elsewhere. Of course, no official record exists to confirm this.

About two weeks after Mirella's arrest, I stepped out of work one evening for a quick stroll, only to stumble into a small park packed full of mounted police officers, 60 in all. Riots had returned to Brixton, transforming streets into battle zones and, after four days, the police had had enough. I recognised a detective and asked him what was going on. 'The mounties are going to baton charge the rioters,' he explained. Thanking him, I hurried away, turning around and heading back to work. Such an action would invite a bloodbath. As soon as I arrived at the mortuary I set about making sure that everything was in good order, as I feared we might soon be facing the arrival of several bodies of young black men, victims of police officers given carte blanche to do whatever it took to restore order.

The riots had started after an early-morning police raid on a Brixton flat by the CID. They were after a suspect called Michael Groce because he'd waved a gun at one of their officers. The raid was led by Inspector Douglas Lovelock, an authorised firearms officer (AFO). At the time there were 3,000 or so AFOs in the Metropolitan Police. At his trial, he told the court that he just saw 'a shape coming towards me … and a shot rang out.' He'd shot Cherry Groce, Michael's mother, while she was in her bed, leaving her paralysed from the chest down. Lovelock was acquitted of all charges. Michael, who was already in hiding in his sister's flat, didn't find out until several days later when he switched on the TV. He immediately turned himself in.

Following the shooting of Cherry Groce, an angry crowd gathered outside the Groce house and the press swarmed into Brixton. By the afternoon, an uprising had started, and the *Sunday Telegraph* sent 29-year-old David Hodge to cover the situation. A freelance photographer who specialised in science photography, it was his first assignment for the paper. Wanting to broaden his experience, he'd pinned his business card to the wall next to the picture desk in the paper's office. For major events that required more photographers than were on staff, picture editors turned to the wall and contacted whoever was available.

Street sense was everything; reporters and photographers

dodged in and out of the rioters and police lines hoping that adrenaline would continue to suppress fear. Hodge took pictures of youths trying to break into the jewellers in the Reliance Arcade on Brixton Road. As he moved closer, he was jumped and beaten up by at least eight men, and his camera gear was stolen. Passers-by saved him and took him to King's College Hospital. He was discharged after 48 hours, but ten days later I arrived in the mortuary to find David's body on the PM table.

The cause of death turned out to have been a blood clot caused by injuries sustained during his beating. The subsequent trial of an eighteen-year-old security guard, Elroy Palmer, collapsed because the jury couldn't agree on a verdict. The second trial failed, and Palmer moved to Australia. David had been medically trained, and was especially interested in heart transplants. His heart was donated to a doctor, who lived for another ten years. His family and friends set up the David Hodge Award for photojournalists under 30, currently sponsored by the *Observer*.

The 1985 riots, coming during a wave of civil unrest, and just after the miners' strike, led to a politicisation of Britain's poor, a national resentment of the police, and to Thatcher's more disastrous hard-line stances. A review of Met gun policy after Cherry Groce's shooting resulted in a ban on CID detectives carrying firearms.

All of this did nothing to lessen racial tensions. Some months later, when Mirella's trial took place at the Old Bailey, someone had scrawled in chalk on a pillar in front of the courthouse: 'Burn the black cunt.'

THE ISSUE FOR the jury was whether Mirella had *intended* to kill the children and, if she had, whether she was suffering an abnormality of mind that diminished her responsibility at the time. There was no question that Mirella, by now receiving treatment for her psychiatric illness, regretted what she had done. Speaking to the court, she said: 'I loved her [Tina] so much. I am now childless. I do not even want to see another day. It is like a nightmare to me. I cannot believe she is not here with me or never will be again. I close my eyes. I can see them both in white lace. Two little angels smiling with me. Without my Tina it is very painful. It is like two big crosses – that is something I have to face. Tina will always be in my heart forever and ever until the day we meet in heaven.'

Denying Mirella her insanity plea, the jury found her guilty of murder and the judge gave her two life sentences.

Missing boy Barry Lewis' body was discovered a year later in Epping Forest, the victim of a paedophile ring. Two men were eventually found guilty of his killing; one was murdered in prison, the other was shot dead on his doorstep shortly after his release.

There was one silver lining to all this, however, and it came some months later, unexpectedly, from Wendy. She arrived home one evening after another long shift and poured us both a large glass of wine. 'You know what I did today?', she asked. I shook my head and shrugged.

'I helped Stacey Kavanagh's mother give birth to a perfectly healthy child.'

12

Little Legs

September 1985

I was at my desk late one afternoon when the phone rang. A very excited funeral director was on the line and, after telling him to slow down and repeat what he was trying to tell me, I realised that we had made a dreadful error.

The funeral director, whose name was Henry, was in his sixties and had been in the business well over 30 years. He was a short, cheerful man and always had time for a chat, displaying nothing but consummate care and professionalism. He was just the sort of man I'd like to handle my own funeral.

A few days previously, we had handed over the body of 79-year-old gentleman into his care. The deceased's family had asked for a cremation at Honour Oak Crematorium, a tranquil building known for its magnificent stained-glass window. Forty people were expected to attend.

'Today was supposed to be the cremation,' he told me.

'Supposed?'

'Everything was going fine until the coffin went into the cremator. About a minute later, there was a bang, followed by another and then a *huge* explosion!'

Apparently smoke had filled the chapel and the mourners had dashed out in a panic. A technician had to be taken to hospital with minor injuries while two others were treated for shock. After clearing the cemetery, the fire brigade moved in for a closer look. On putting out the fire they could see that it was the half-burned body that had exploded. Further searching revealed the components of a pacemaker – the cause of the explosion. This in turn created a panic because a new breed of nuclear-powered pacemakers had recently been launched; the catchily-named Radioisotope Thermoelectric Generator Pacemakers (RTGPs). Although no one would ever need one to run that long, these plutonium-powered pacemakers would apparently keep going for at least a thousand years. This longevity saved the patient the trauma, and the NHS the expense, of surgical battery replacement.

Plutonium is one of the most dangerous materials in the world and so numerous layers and shields were woven into the pacemakers, ensuring zero radiation leakage. The armour was tough enough to resist a gunshot at point-blank range. After an explosion like this, however, no one seemed to know whether there would be any public risk.

'So, as no one knew what type of pacemaker he had, they used a Geiger counter,' Henry continued. 'All hell broke loose when the thing started making a loud, rapid clicking noise. The fire brigade started pushing people back before the crematorium manager admitted that he'd had one of the nuclear pacemakers fitted a year ago! That's what the Geiger counter was picking up! Thank goodness that the gentleman who'd exploded had the old type.'

Fire investigators later found a finger-sized hole half an inch deep in the cremator wall. Among the remains, there were five discs, a short length of wire and a metal plate. The device was identified as a zinc-mercuric oxide pacemaker. It had exploded thanks to the rapid formation of hydrogen gas, which had burst the casing. The crematorium was going to be out of action for at least a week, but fortunately the stained-glass window escaped shrapnel damage.

'The best part though,' Henry said, 'came when I went to apologise to the deceased's wife, a lovely little old lady. I said sorry over and over, but she waved my apologies away. She was even smiling. She said: "That's alright, my Gerald always said he wanted to go out with a bang."'

Professor Mant had conducted the PM, but none of us had spotted the pacemaker. This, it turned out, was not that unusual. Pacemakers can move about inside the body. One report into the matter, called 'A Migrating Pacemaker', told the story of a doctor who found a pacemaker buried deep in the muscle of the chest, about ten centimetres from where it was supposed to be. It suggested that metal detectors be used to avoid explosions in crematoria, of which, we were also surprised to learn, there had already been a great many.

Such explosions occur even today. A 2012 survey of the 71 UK crematoria that had reported pacemaker explosions during the previous year found that 30 per cent had suffered significant damage. In 3 per cent of cases, the crematoria had been damaged beyond repair.

Soon after our own pacemaker explosion, two questions were added to Form B of the government-mandated Cremation Act Certificate, which a doctor fills out prior to a cremation: '(a) Has a pacemaker or any radioactive material been inserted in the deceased (yes or no)?; (b) If so, has it been removed (yes or no)?'

I'm sure that you will be relieved to know that modern technology has led to the development of non-nuclear powered pacemakers, so today there is very little risk of a mushroom cloud rising above your local crematorium. Having said that, although no accidental cremations of nuclear pacemakers have occurred as yet, there remains a handful of people still walking around with plutonium-powered pacemakers in their chests.

As soon as I placed the receiver back in its cradle after speaking with Henry, the phone rang again. A murder was waiting for me in the PM room. Professor Johnson was already there, a ball of furious energy as usual as he impatiently waited for me to set up. A detective I hadn't met before was with him. He was a huge man wearing a long raincoat, smoking a Superkings cigarette. He dwarfed his two colleagues as he stepped forward, holding out a huge hand, introducing himself as DCI O'Connor from a police division in Lambeth.

The body on the slab belonged to a short middle-aged man, not more than five feet in height. He was naked and

Exterior view of Southwark Mortuary.

Peter Everett with the contents of his murder bag.

Foul room at Southwark Mortuary.

(LEFT) Old fridge store area, Southwark Mortuary, before renovations took place.

Post-mortem room at St Mary's Hospital Mortuary, Paddington.

'BODIES FOR SALE' CLAIM

by JOHN TWOMEY

A BATTERSEA coroner's officer has been suspended after allegations of bribery between policemen and undertakers.

He is PC ████████, who worked in the coroner's court in Sheepcote Lane, Battersea.

Another coroner's officer — PC ████████ from Croydon coroner's court — retired from the force on Monday as the investigation was being carried out.

The claim is that some coroners' officers have taken bribes from undertakers for putting them in touch with bereaved families.

And the probe is believed to centre on a firm of funeral directors with branches in the Clapham and Tooting areas.

It was launched by Scotland Yard's Complaints Investigation Bureau after allegations were made by the London Association of Funeral Directors.

Spokesman Ivor Leverton said: "There is one firm in South London which was particularly worrying our association.

"That firm seemed to be getting preferential treatment. It has been worrying us for about the last two or three years."

One Wandsworth funeral director said most firms in the area knew which firm is at the centre of the allegations.

He said, "We all very much welcome the police investigation."

He added that every funeral director in the area had been visited by police in search of information about the firm.

Scotland Yard have refused to discuss details of the investigation which is being headed by Deputy Assistant Commissioner James Sewell and Commander Michael Taylor.

'"BODIES FOR SALE" CLAIM', *South London Press*, Friday 22 October 1982, front page story.

Glands sold for 25p, mortuary chief says

Mr Peter Everett, superintendent of Southwark mortuary in south London, yesterday told Southwark Crown Court that there were corrupt mortuaries all over the country.

On the third day of the trial of a man charged with conspiring to steal from corpses, Mr Everett said there were both "legitimate" and "non-legitimate" fiddles.

Examples of the legitimate fiddles, he told the court, were the measuring of bodies for undertakers, for which mortuary assistants would take tips from undertakers and the removing of pituitary glands from the brains of corpses.

The court was told a pituitary gland would fetch about 25p when sold for medical research. Mr Everett said that it was not unusual for illegal transactions to take place at mortuaries. "It is well known throughout the country that there are a lot of corrupt mortuaries," he said.

████████, aged 18, a mortuary assistant, faces a charge of conspiracy to steal from the Borough of Southwark between November, 1981, and October, 1982. He also denies inciting Mr Everett to steal property from the borough.

The trial was adjourned until Monday.

Scandal of 'gem thefts from dead'

BY SUN REPORTER

THE DEAD are being stripped of valuables in a widespread corruption racket in morgues, a court heard yesterday.

Crooked staff steal rings and jewellery, mortuary superintendent Peter Everett alleged. They even make cash by selling off glands from the bodies, he said

"The dead do not rest in peace. There is much money to be had," Mr Everett told Southwark Crown Court, South London.

"It is renowned that throughout the country there are a lot of corrupt mortuaries."

Mr Everett, 36, was giving evidence against Southwark Mortuary assistant ████████, 18, of Peckham, who denies conspiracy to steal. The trial continues.

(FAR LEFT) 'Glands sold for 25p, mortuary chief says', *The Times*, 1983.

(LEFT) 'Scandal of "gem thefts from dead"', *The Times*, 1983.

BODY CASH SNATCH CASE

Mortuary worker is charged with stealing jewellery

A MORTUARY'S deputy supervisor who is charged with stripping bodies of jewellery and cash has been remanded on unconditional bail.

████████ (25), allegedly stole property worth £1,000 from three bodies at Southwark Mortuary, by Southwark Coroners' Court, Tennis Street, Borough.

At Tower Bridge magistrates' court on Monday she was also accused of forging entries in the mortuary property book.

She is accused of three charges of theft, one of forging and one of false accounting between March 21 and November 30 last year and was remanded until October 5.

████████ who has one child, was suspended from her job after her arrest in March this year.

'BODY CASH SNATCH CASE',
South London Press, Friday 28 August 1987.

Woman stole from bodies

HEARTLESS gold digger ████████ stole cash and jewellery from dead bodies on the mortuary slab.

The Southwark mortuary attendant rifled cash, jewellery, credit cards, rings, a Rotary watch and cheque books worth a total of £1,000 from three corpses.

The 25-year-old admitted the ghoulish crime at Inner London Crown Court.

She carried out the thefts at Southwark mortuary in Tennis Street. The offences date back to 1985.

She stripped at least one body and lifted other personal possessions from the mortuary safe before passing on some of the goods to her husband ████████ (28) who has admitted handling stolen goods worth £260.

████████ was also charged with falsifying mortuary accounts in connection with the theft and of forgery.

She denied false accounting and three other counts of theft, but admits three thefts and one forgery.

████████ was sentenced to 21 months imprisonment, nine months suspended. Her husband was sentenced to 12 months. The not guilty pleas were left

'Woman stole from bodies',
South London Press, Friday 15 April 1988.

Man 'robbed corpses'

Cash and jewelry were stripped from bodies in a London mortuary by two unscrupulous assistants, Southwark Crown Court was told yesterday.

No sooner had undertakers delivered the corpses than their pockets were rifled and rings and watches removed Mr Francis Evans, alleged for the prosecution. He added: "This is a rather horrible and bizarre story."

"They stole only from bodies with little or no family concern." ████████ who is giving evidence against ████████ his former colleague at Southwark Mortuary told the court that they often took property from corpses which were highly decomposed.

████████, aged 18, of Hollydale Road, Peckham, south east London, denies conspiring with ████████ to steal from The London Borough of Southwark between November, 1981, and October, 1982. He also denies inciting the mortuary superintendent to steal property.

'Man "robbed corpses"', *The Times*, 1984.

Ghoul stole from dead

MORTUARY attendant ████████ was yesterday jailed for 18 months, nine suspended, for robbing the dead.

He stripped cash and jewellery from bodies as they lay on his slab.

And Judge Edward Fox told ████████ at Southwark Crown Court: "These are grave offences."

████████, 26, of Gurridge Road, Waterloo, South London, admitted conspiracy and incitement to steal, theft and handling stolen coffins.

'Ghoul stole from dead',
The Daily Star,
19 January 1984.

had clearly suffered a huge trauma to the back of his head. Glancing at the body as I gathered the buckets, I could see brain matter in the man's hair.

'Shot at point-blank range,' DCI O'Connor said, 'while naked in bed, about midnight last night. This is, or was, Brian "Little Legs" Clifford, 44 years old and a right evil villain if ever there was one.'

This was the first underworld assassination I'd seen, which was surprising really considering that South London in the 1980s was a hotbed of criminal activity, packed with bank robbers, thieves, fences, fraudsters and drug dealers, most of whom weren't afraid of firing the odd bullet or ten if they thought it would further their cause.

'Mr Clifford here,' O'Connor continued as Professor Johnson made the first incision, 'was up to his eyeballs in criminality. He ran a few West End nightclubs, but they were just a front really; he bought and sold stolen gear at the highest level: everything from TVs to jewellery. He wasn't afraid of a ruckus either; he shot an Irish mobster by the name of Johnny Mangan twice in the head in 1979. He survived and Little Legs here was charged with attempted murder, but the clever little bastard got off on a technicality.'

'What was the technicality?' I asked.

'A bloody expensive lawyer.'

As Professor Johnson and I worked, DCI O'Connor continued to regale us with stories about Little Legs' criminal activities, including the time he travelled to Switzerland with thousands in forged US dollars, successfully swapping them for genuine British currency at an international bank. He was also well-known to 'Mad' Frankie Fraser, an old-school criminal who began his career by burgling people's homes while they were hiding from German bombing raids in the Second World War. He later became known for torturing his fellow gangsters by pulling out their teeth with a rusty pair of pliers. Perhaps not surprisingly, by the end of his career, Mad Frankie had spent 42 years of his life in prison, earning his 'Mad' sobriquet after he assaulted a prison governor and was sent to Broadmoor. Mad Frankie said he often used Little Legs Clifford as a fence.

Little Legs, a handsome man with wavy black hair had, like Mad Frankie, an uncontrollable temper and enjoyed violence. No one dared refer to his height, or lack of it. He was so short that he had to fasten wooden blocks to his feet so he could reach the pedals of his Rolls Royce.

He lived with his wife and son in a large Victorian house in Kennington Road. By all accounts, he was not the best of fathers and, after his assassination, his sixteen-year-old son Bernie's first concern was to retrieve a pair of Pierre Cardin shoes from the bedroom where his father's body was lying. Bernie, who inherited his father's stature, went on to become a legendary manager of celebrity haunt the Groucho Club, and was crowned 'The Prince of Soho' by Stephen Fry before his own sudden and untimely death in 2017, aged just 49.

Bernie had once described his father as 'a real villain with a heavy clout around South London', and this was borne out by the detectives dealing with his case, for there were rumours that he was, to a limited extent, involved in the aftermath of that decade's most notorious robbery.

If you wanted to become an armed robber, or needed guns for hire or men for a 'job', then from the 70s through to the late 80s, the Downham Tavern on Downham Way near the Old Kent Road was the place to go. In the autumn of 1983, a job that would change South London for ever was punted around the bar by young hard man and blagger (bank robber) Micky McAvoy, who wanted some heavies for a raid on the Brink's-Mat Warehouse at Heathrow. He found no shortage of willing accomplices, including a well-connected old blagger called Brian Robinson and, a few weeks later, just after 6.40am on 26 November 1983, six armed men charged into the warehouse, quickly disabled the sophisticated security system, tied up the guards, doused them with petrol and threatened to set them alight unless they revealed the combination to the huge vault.

McAvoy had heard there would be £3 million in cash in the vault. Instead, it was full of gold. They left with 6,800 gold bars worth £26 million. It was the UK's biggest ever criminal haul. Once the gold market heard the news, it panicked, causing the stolen gold to rise in value by another million.

Fifteen days after the robbery, on 11 December, a man in his late thirties strolled down Hatton Garden – the undisputed centre of Britain's gold and diamond trade – before entering Charles Cooper Ltd at number 8. The man, speaking in a strong cockney accent, said that he was after an industrial gold smelter. He was told that it would be possible to get a machine that liquefied 36 kilograms at a time. 'That'll do nicely,' the man said. He wanted to take it with him there and then, but this was impossible as it had to be ordered.

Following this visit, the shop manager, suspecting the obvious, called the Flying Squad (a specialist unit unique to London that deals with armed and unarmed robberies) and, after looking through a book of mugshots, he picked out a face that turned out to be a friend of McAvoy. This was the Flying Squad's first real lead. Detectives started following McAvoy and then Robinson – noting that they'd both left their council houses for enormous homes in Kent, paid for in cash. McAvoy had also bought two Rottweiler dogs and named them Brinks and Mat.

Then detectives found out that security guard Tony Black had been the inside man. Black told all and fingered McAvoy in the police line-up. McAvoy head-butted him in response (this was in the days before identity parades were conducted with a one-way glass partition between suspect and witness). McAvoy and Robinson ended up with 25 years apiece. The gold proved much harder to find with only £16 million of the original £26 million so far recovered.

After his arrest, Micky McAvoy asked his friends and fellow criminals Brian Perry and George Francis to look after his cut so it would be waiting for him when he got out. McAvoy also offered the police his share of the gold for a reduction in his 25-year sentence.

Perry responded with: 'Once the cell door's closed, what's he got to trade?', implying that neither he nor Francis were about to hand over any gold to help McAvoy get out of jail.

McAvoy wrote Perry a letter: 'You're signing your own death warrant. I have no intention of being fucked for my money here and still do this sentence. Give my love to your family, mate. Take care. All the best, Micky.'

Brian Perry ignored the threat and turned out to be an astute property developer when he invested some of his golden profits in cheap wasteland out in the Docklands. A few years later, in 1988, the construction of Canary Wharf made him a multi-millionaire.

Meanwhile, in the years immediately following Brink's-Mat, the police were hunting everywhere for the gold, and they suspected that some of it had been steered between sources by the fencing fingers of Brian Little Legs Clifford, whose well-established smuggling networks were second to none.

And that brings us to the curse of Brink's-Mat. Since the robbery, nine men involved in the job have been murdered, not counting Little Legs.

Brian Perry was shot three times in the back of the head while George Francis, who once said, 'I would rather die quickly by the bullet than slowly in some old people's home that stinks of cabbage water,' got his wish when two gunmen shot him four times as he was opening the door to his Rover.

Mad Frankie wrote in his memoir that everyone in South London knew it was 'coming on top' for Little Legs (i.e. his life was in danger), except him. And that brings us to the truly mysterious manner of his death.

To help the profs and myself visualise the scene and understand the sequence of events and, therefore, the manner of someone's murder, I often made a sketch of the scene as a detective described it to me. And this scene beggared more questions than answers.

As DCI O'Connor explained, at around midnight Little Legs was fast asleep in his bed. His wife and a couple of friends were enjoying a drink downstairs when the doorbell rang. Mrs Clifford opened the door to be confronted by a man in a balaclava armed with a shotgun. Pushing her aside, the gunman ran upstairs and shot Clifford in the back of the head and quickly ran back out into the night.

As I sketched the scene, tracking the route of the killer through the house, a question entered my mind. How did the gunman know exactly where to find Little Legs? He must have known that he was asleep and in his bedroom. Who told him?

And then we learned that for two weeks, a police surveillance unit had been keeping a 24-hour watch on Clifford's home. The night of his assassination was the first time in fourteen days that the police had not been present.

To this day, more than £10 million from the robbery is still unaccounted for. No one was ever prosecuted for Little Legs's murder. A straightforward cause of death for us, but another frustrating piece of the Brink's-Mat puzzle for Scotland Yard.

13

The Stockwell Strangler

June 1986

3am, 27 June 1986

The heatwave baking London dry for the last month or so had been relentless, with night-time temperatures barely dropping below 25 degrees Celsius. Seventy-three-year-old Fred Prentice had been struggling to sleep when he heard footsteps coming from the corridor outside of his room. Fred, a small, wiry man who needed two canes to walk, lived on the first floor of Bradmead, an old people's home, on Cedars Road, Clapham. His room faced away from the street and was on the first floor, so he hadn't thought twice about leaving the windows open. Besides, the home was staffed 24 hours a day. Looking up, he saw a shadow flash past the mottled glass of his bedroom door, return a moment later and then pause. He sat up as his bedroom door started to open.

The figure moved into the room. Fred reached over to turn on his bedside lamp but the figure jumped onto the bed, grabbing him by the shoulders, forcing him onto his back.

Fred tried to cry out but his attacker clamped a hand over his mouth and put his knees on Fred's chest. Wide-eyed with terror, Fred stared into the grinning face of a young man with dark hair. The man put a finger to his lips, mockingly indicating that Fred should keep quiet, and then reached for Fred's throat. Fred thrashed and tried to scream but he quickly became dizzy, at which point his attacker loosened his grip, prolonging his enjoyment, as Fred gasped for air. Staring into Fred's terrified eyes, the young man quietly repeated 'Kill, kill, kill', over and over again. Not all Fred's strength had left him, however, and he twisted wildly under the crazed man's grip the next time he loosened it, throwing out an arm and this time having the good fortune to hit the panic button that was just above his headboard. The noise of the alarm and the harsh sound of a telephone, alerting the warden to a possible heart attack, was enough to scare the attacker away, but not before he picked Fred up and threw him against the wall.

9am, 28 June 1986

The PM room, with its thick walls and stone floor, was one of the few places in London that remained pleasantly cool for at least part of the day. Professor Hugh Johnson, dressed in green scrubs, was snapping on surgical gloves while DCS Graham Melvin, a tall, plain-looking man who was a no-nonsense, old-school detective, stared at the two frail bodies lying on the PM tables before him. Also present were two nameless detectives, both smoking, wearing plain, worka-day suits.

'Eighty-four-year-old Valentine Gleim, a former British Army officer,' Melvin said quietly, pointing to the body to the left, 'and 94-year-old Polish-born Zbigniew Strabawa.'

They looked so tiny and frail lying on the enamel slabs, especially with all these tall men standing around them.

'They were neighbours in a council care home,' Melvin continued. Pat started to arrange the buckets on the PM tables while I combed the men's thin hair, giving them both a centre parting in preparation for dissection. 'Somerville Hastings House in Stockwell Park Crescent.'

I couldn't help but notice one of the detectives flinch as my blade pierced the skin covering the skull. Professor Johnson leaned in, looking at the bruising on both men's chests, already X-raying the body with keen pathologist's eyes.

'They lived in neighbouring rooms and were best friends. Both of them were found in bed. The killer got in through an open window. The night duty nurses became suspicious at 4am, when they heard someone using an electric razor, and saw the shadow of an intruder in the corridor. They called the police but the man vanished by the time officers arrived.'

'Why the electric razor?' I asked. Melvin looked at me, shrugged and replied deadpan: 'Because the killer needed a shave. He had a wash too. A freshly-used flannel was lying in the basin in Strabawa's en-suite.'

'We have a witness,' he added. 'He tried it on the night before but the victim, Fred Prentice, managed to hit his panic button. Mr Prentice's description of the man matches that given by the nurses at Somerville House, although it's not much: in his twenties, with dark hair.'

Professor Johnson had a quick look at the dissected head before beginning the PM proper, starting with the exterior examination. 'In all cases of neck compression there are definitive post-mortem signs,' he said before pointing out the petechial haemorrhages: small dark spots the size of a pinhead, commonly found behind the ears, easily missed by the untrained eye. As the dissection of the bodies continued, Professor Johnson pointed out the fractured hyoid bone in both cases. The hyoid is a tiny stirrup-shaped bone with two horns which sits under the lower jaw. Someone gripping the neck strongly enough to asphyxiate inevitably fractures the horns, making diagnosis conclusive. As the PM progressed we learned – thanks to tears to his anus, from which we extracted samples of semen – that Gleim had been sexually assaulted as well as being strangled.

'Most of their ribs are fractured,' Professor Johnson said. 'Most likely, the killer attacked while they were still asleep. He kneeled on their chests, and from bruising to the mouth I'd say he clamped their mouths shut with his left hand and strangled them with his right. They would have fallen unconscious in 30 seconds and died within two or three minutes.'

'Stabbings and blunt instruments I see every week,' Professor Johnson continued, removing his surgical gloves. 'I might see a strangling once every five years. It's an inefficient way to kill somebody. It takes a long time, and when a person is fighting for their life, they can summon up huge reserves of strength.'

Professor Johnson paused for a moment, glancing at me and I could tell from that look what he was about to say next. 'And we've seen another strangling of an elderly person just a few weeks ago.'

On 9 June a pair of detectives had arrived at Southwark Mortuary with the naked body of 67-year-old Janet Cockett. Recently widowed, Janet was chairperson of her tenants' association. She was also popular with her neighbours and by all accounts had led an active life. She had four children from three marriages and a bunch of grandchildren. She lived in a first floor flat in Warwick House, a low-rise council block on the Overton Road Estate in Stockwell.

'It didn't look suspicious at first,' one of the detectives said. 'She was in bed with the sheets pulled up under her chin. But Mrs Cockett had dozens of framed photos of her kids, grandkids and hubby in her bedroom,' he continued. 'They'd all been turned around to face the wall or laid face down. Her nightdress was folded neatly on a stool next to her bed. When I lifted it up it was torn; clearly it had been ripped from her body.'

It was obvious to me that Janet had suffered a violent death. Severe bruises covered her chest and abdomen. Leaning in a little closer, I could see marks on her throat and tiny spots of blood under the skin behind her ears, bruising from where the killer's fingertips would have pressed into her skin. Professor Johnson pointed these injuries out to the photographer and then, after we'd lifted her onto the table, he cut the Y incision and peeled back the flesh of her chest to reveal broken ribs. Pulling and slicing away flesh and muscle upwards, towards Janet's face, Professor Johnson stopped and motioned the photographer closer for another picture. 'Broken hyoid bone,' he said and Pat made the relevant note on the PM form.

UPON HEARING THIS story, Melvin nodded quietly, glanced at the two detectives and then said: 'There was another one. Two months ago, in April. You wouldn't have seen her; she was dealt with at Wandsworth.

'Seventy-eight-year-old retired schoolteacher Nancy Emms. A recluse. Never married. Lived alone in a run-down basement flat. Suffered from mild dementia. The home help found Nancy lying dead in bed with the covers tucked under her chin. It seemed as though Nancy had died in her sleep and her doctor registered the death as natural causes. But then it was noticed that Nancy's portable TV was missing. No sign of forced entry, but a window was open. She was strangled and sexually assaulted.'

'Any clues for either of the cases?' I asked.

'A hair on the bed of Emms and a palm print on Cockett's window.'

Matching the print – if a match existed – would take time, as the search of the 4 million prints on the police files had to be performed manually. Computerisation wasn't due to begin until the following year, so prints tended to prove useful only after the suspect had been captured. To me, even with my limited experience (and I would never dream of telling a police detective how to do their job, not for as long as I wanted to stay in mine), it was obvious that we had a serial killer on our hands. I knew that stranger murders were rare (most murder victims knew their killer) and that as far as methods went, strangling, especially with bare hands, was even rarer. For two different murderers to have killed two pensioners who lived just five kilometres apart, at roughly the same time of night in the same way and both with a sexual element (Janet hadn't been raped but she had been stripped of her nightie), well that seemed like long odds indeed. Now, with these two poor old fellows, there could be no question.

Four strangulations of old persons in just eleven weeks, the intervals between each attack decreasing. That only meant one thing – he would strike again soon, and the hot weather would provide him with more than enough opportunities. 'Not a word to the press,' Melvin ordered. 'We'll make a statement soon enough, but for now we're going to see how far we can get before we go public and possibly scare the killer off to another part of the country.'

Fortunately for Melvin, the press was swamped with major news stories that summer, what with several child abductions in Suffolk, the Chernobyl disaster and Prince Andrew and Sarah Ferguson's wedding just weeks away.

While Pat and I debated the merits of warning the public, dozens of plain-clothed officers staked out old people's homes throughout South London, and we braced ourselves for the arrival of the next victim. We wouldn't have long to wait.

ON 20 JULY, I was looking down at the frail body of another pensioner. The strangler had returned to the Overton Estate where he'd previously murdered Janet Cockett. This time the victim was male: 74-year-old William Downes, who, according to his neighbours, kept himself to himself, rarely leaving his small studio flat – the low-rise kind that the killer preferred. His son had found him: 'I told him, I warned him to keep his door and windows locked, especially at night, but it was hot and I think he left just one slightly open to let some air in.'

Melvin again sat in on the PM and, once Professor Johnson had confirmed that Downes had been strangled, he sighed and prepared to leave: 'I'm going to talk to the press this afternoon, so prepare to be under siege. Do not talk to them and do not let anyone into the mortuary unless they work here, right?'

Newspaper stories had already started to appear, referencing the 'Stockwell Strangler', as all but two of the murders had taken place in that area. Melvin gave his press conference. 'We know that the killer strikes between 1am and 3am in low-rise blocks of flats where the elderly live.'

'Do you have a suspect?' a journalist asked.

'We are pursuing a number of leads and we are looking for a young white male with short dark hair and a sun-tanned face who is local to the Stockwell area.'

'So not much then!'

Among the other leads the police were pursuing was the possibility that the strangler might be working in the area as a postman or milkman; that he was an experienced burglar (albeit with little forensic awareness – two more palm prints that matched those found at the first murder had been recovered from Downes' flat) and may have a criminal record. The search for a match continued. There was also the possibility that he had a history of mental illness with the rare condition of gerontophilia (sexual desire for the elderly) and that looking at medical records could help to reveal his identity.

A psychologist was brought in to try to profile the killer. He seized on the killings as expressions of love because of the way the attacker had sex with the victims and arranged the bodies. Apart from the fact that it was very likely that he'd been institutionalised, and that warning signs of his behaviour had been present for months, if not years before the first murder, the police still had precious little to go on.

Pensioners were understandably terrified, thanks in part to the *Sun* newspaper, who described a 'faceless monster', before plastering a terrifying 'artist's impression' of the killer's face across its inside pages. Help the Aged ran ads offering advice and started a helpline while detectives patrolled the streets. The strangler was a classic serial killer. The time between killings was shortening. There was a ritual. A particular victim type.

On 23 July the entire country was watching the royal wedding of Sarah Ferguson and Prince Andrew. The following morning, a few pages into the Sunday papers, after masses of wedding pictures, I saw that the Stockwell Strangler had struck again. This time in Putney, which was beyond my mortuary's borders. Florence Tisdall, 83, who was partially blind and deaf and walked with a Zimmer frame, had left one of the windows of her ground floor flat open so her three cats could come and go in the night. The killer had raped her, and had broken her ribs as he strangled her. Not mentioned in the paper, because they didn't know, was the fact that the killer had undressed Florence's body – she had still been wearing her day clothes when he attacked her – and redressed her in her nightie before tucking her up. The other difference was that he'd struck earlier in the night but had been helped by the noise coming from a royal wedding disco in the Eight Bells pub just opposite.

A few days later, the tireless workers from the finger-print department finally found a match: 24-year-old Kenneth Erskine, a schizophrenic drifter. A check of benefits offices revealed that Erskine collected his dole check every second Monday from Keyworth House, a short distance from the mortuary, where staff knew him as 'the whisperer' because he was so softly spoken. Sure enough, on the next Monday Erskine arrived on time and offered no resistance as detectives picked him up.

KENNETH ERSKINE, THE eldest of four children, was born to Margaret and Charles in Hammersmith on 1 July 1962. His parents divorced in the mid-70s, by which time Erskine and his brothers had already spent several months in care homes or with foster parents. His neighbours remembered him as a cheerful, chubby boy, often reading the Bible, and claiming to believe in love and peace. After the divorce he turned into a bully, attacking smaller children for no reason, sometimes tying them up. Erskine was expelled from a series of specialist schools for a number of offences. He stabbed a teacher through the hand with a pair of scissors; took a psychiatric nurse hostage, holding a pair of scissors to her throat; pushed a fellow pupil off a moving bus, and almost burned down one of his schools. He also attempted to drown several children on a trip to a swimming pool by holding their heads underwater until staff intervened. Neither discipline nor affection worked; in fact Erskine was known to respond to affection by rubbing himself against the person in a sexual manner, or by masturbating. At home, he gave his younger brothers cannabis and tried to lynch them. When Erskine was just sixteen, his mother kicked him out of his home. He lived in a series of squats in Brixton and Stockwell, where he began drinking and using hard drugs, turning to burglary for money. Arrested several times, Erskine ended up in Feltham Young Offenders' Institution where he whiled away the time drawing and painting. His cellmate, a burglar named James Doel, recalled that Erskine's pictures were of elderly people who were bound and gagged, stabbed, burned and decapitated. Against doctors' advice, Erskine was released in 1982 and returned to his previous ways. He made no friends, had no possessions and never stayed anywhere for long.

During police interviews Erskine admitted burgling the old people's homes, but claimed that someone else followed him in after he'd left each time, and they must have killed the pensioners. He then changed his story, and said that he didn't remember killing anyone, but that he may have done so without knowing it. Gísli Guðjónsson, CBE, Professor of

Forensic Psychology at the Institute of Psychiatry at King's College London, was asked to evaluate Erskine's fitness for trial. 'He didn't communicate very well,' he said in his conclusion. 'He denied there was anything wrong with him. I wired him up to a machine that allowed me to monitor his sweat response, asked him sensitive questions, and his autonomic reactions told me he understood enough to go on trial.'*

A simple end to what had become a desperate hunt. But, as I would soon find out, this was far from the end of the strangler's story. A few days later, I was in my office, trying to sort through a tonne of files, arranging them in a ring binder, and was trying to clear a space in which to work but ended up tipping over a great stack of paperwork. As I stooped to gather it up, I stopped. A single word had caught my eye: strangulation. John Jordan, 57. Found dead in his flat in Brixton on 4 February. He was younger than Erskine's other victims, but I wondered. I decided to look through the files for further cases of strangulation or suffocation, and it wasn't long before I found more.

Other recent cases of strangulation included 73-year-old Charles Quarrell, suffocated at his home in Southwark on 6 May, and 70-year-old Wilfred Parkes, strangled in his bedroom on the Stockwell Park Estate on 28 May. Although these had taken place on our patch, they had been transferred

---

* Erskine was sentenced to an indefinite period in a psychiatric institution but, in 2009, his medical team at Broadmoor led an appeal to have his conviction for murder replaced by manslaughter. They were successful and in 2016 Erskine was moved to a medium secure hospital unit. Now 66 years old, Erskine could be released any day.

to other mortuaries because on those days we were operating beyond capacity. These, added to the suspected case of 75-year-old Trevor Thomas, whose body was found in an advanced state of decomposition in his home in Clapham, 12 July, would bring the killer's count to eleven, thus far. Perhaps these investigations were quietly closed because the police were certain they had found their killer. I'm still haunted by the thought that the Strangler might have claimed more victims beyond Southwark's borders.

14

Cleaning up

July–September 1986

I arrived for work somewhat distracted, the thoughts of the Stockwell Strangler's other victims still playing on my mind. Stepping into the PM room, however, this was immediately driven from my mind by our latest arrival: a skeleton, which was being examined by Professor Johnson.

'We don't see many of those,' I commented, leaning in and taking a closer look. 'It doesn't even look that old.'

'It isn't,' Professor Johnson replied. He was smiling, which was unusual for him, especially first thing in the morning. 'A member of the public found it at the back of the car park of the National Theatre. Probably a vagrant.'

He was chuckling to himself as he examined the body.

'What's so funny?' I asked.

His chuckles increased until, trying to stifle a guffaw, the normally grumpy pathologist finally managed to splutter:

'The National Theatre fired their car park attendant on the spot!'

He continued giggling for the entire length of the skeleton's PM, and Pat and I couldn't help but join in. Laughter, however macabre its origin, was a pleasure to hear in these dark times.

After the unusually cheerful Professor Johnson had left, Pat wheeled in the next body, that of a 30-something-year-old man. It was a misshapen mess of flesh, still intact, but it looked as though all the bones had been removed.

'Goodness, me, what on earth happened here?' I asked.

'He was a stonemason working on the roof of the OXO tower,' Pat replied. 'He stepped back to admire his handiwork and fell through the O.'

I don't know why exactly, but I struggled to contain a wry smile.

SOMETHING THAT HAD been troubling me ever since I'd started work at the mortuary was the poor state of the facilities. It really was time to literally clean things up. The building was filthy and packed with more health hazards than the tomb in *Raiders of the Lost Ark*. Fortunately, the silver lining to my courtroom cloud two years ago was that the council agreed that they had to renovate the mortuary. It had taken two years of me reminding them of this agreement until, at long last, planning meetings were held and blueprints drawn up. However, I was not consulted.

Tenders went out and my bosses were invited to attend

a number of long lunches with would-be contractors (it seemed that the banning of extramural inducements didn't apply to senior executives). When the final blueprints were revealed to me I ran a sceptical eye over them. The plans worked on paper but I could see, from a Health and Safety point of view, that they were a biological death trap. I alerted the council, and they chose to ignore me, so I battened down what hatches I could and waited for the proverbial to hit the fan.

An electrical engineer arrived; he normally worked on generators but had been assigned to re-wire the PM room. He ran a 50-metre wire from the junction box to the wall clock. Removing the clock from the wall he discovered that the clock was battery operated! This was only the first of many such gaffs.

Renovations were all very well, but the council had failed to take into account the day-to-day running of the mortuary. We could hardly expect builders, electricians, carpenters, etc., to get on with their work while we dissected bodies. The solution from the council was to hang sheets from a piece of string; this would not halt the pong of 'stinkers' or the smell of bone dust, or the sight of blood trickling across the mortuary floor, nor our gruesome descriptions, nor the ominous sounds of sawing and drilling, but it would at least conceal the worst of the horrific sights.

Most of the workers who turned up did their best to put on a show of bravado and professional detachment, but no one is immune to the horror of death, not least those who have not lived with it for a number of years. I saw the nervous look in their eyes as Pat, Sally and I travelled to and fro, wheeling covered bodies between the fridge area and the PM room.

An added problem was that we seemed to be in the middle of a crime wave and were struggling to find room for all the possible murders along with the many other cases that arrived each day. Things reached a head when on one busy day we took in a stinker along with a macabre murder. The stinker was the body of a woman in her thirties. She had been having a row with her boyfriend, who punched her in the face. She had fallen, cracked her skull on the fireplace and died. The boyfriend went into denial and kept her at home for four days. Each day he would get her out of bed and bathe and dress her. On the fifth day she turned green and he called the police.

Even I was forced to take a sharp intake of breath at the sight of the arrival that followed, hot on the heels of the green lady. No one ever becomes immune to the sight of a body that has come to a particularly brutal end, and myself, Pat, Sally and Professor Mant were no exception. The body had belonged to a 30-something father of three who'd been murdered. We could only imagine the pain he'd been through. As we began the PM, the detectives told us the story – while having to shout over the building work.

'Spare your sympathy,' one of the detectives yelled, looking down at the body, before describing the horrendous abuse the man's wife and children had suffered. 'He was attempting to rape his wife,' the detective continued, 'after he'd beaten her to a pulp. His teenage son, hearing her screams, stepped in to save her and stabbed his father with a pair of scissors, but that wasn't enough. The father grabbed a hammer and chased his son through the house, but not before the son managed to stab him in the chest with a kitchen knife.'

The son had thought that was the end of his father but to his horror, the maniac pulled the knife from his chest and chased the son out of the house and into the back garden.

'The son then grabbed a spade,' the detective continued, 'and smashed his dad over the head with it, but still he wouldn't stop. The son jumped over the garden wall, and that was when his father collapsed and, to make sure he wasn't going to get up, the son dropped a concrete block on his head.'

It was at this point that the string holding up the sheets that surrounded us snapped and half a dozen pale-faced builders found themselves staring down at a man with multiple stab wounds, covered in blood, a pair of scissors protruding from his chest. His face was pulverised by a concrete block, his brain half out of his skull. Next to him was the woman's green and bloated body, her eyes forced open by the swelling.

They walked out, never to return.

The patricidal son faced a trial of manslaughter at the Old Bailey and was placed on probation. As soon as the trial was over, he returned home to his mother.

NONE OF THE pathologists coped very well with the renovations, least of all Professor Johnson, who seemed to be speeding towards a nervous breakdown. The drilling sounded equally loud no matter where you were in the building, as did the sound of workmen yelling at one another, swearing at yet another cock-up or coming across yet another unpleasant sight or smell. After protests from all concerned, the council agreed to allow us to shut up shop for a few weeks and to work out of Lewisham Mortuary. There was only one strict condition from Lewisham: that I didn't go there!

So I stayed, caught up on paperwork and oversaw the works. Things seemed to be going well enough, and then one day something most peculiar occurred. Our old lino floor was ripped out and replaced with orange epoxy. Liquid resin was poured and left to dry overnight. I set the alarms and secured the building, glad to escape the overpowering fumes. The following morning I arrived at work and opened the mortuary door to discover a set of naked footprints imprinted in the dry epoxy floor. They ran in a perfect line from the first mortuary fridge into the post-mortem room, some ten metres in length. It defied explanation; the rooms had high walls and no windows. The footprints only went in one direction. Even a circus trapeze artist couldn't have pulled such a feat off without specialist equipment. No logical explanation was ever found, and after seeing it four of the workmen packed up their tools and refused to come back into the building.

From this moment on, one disaster followed another. Parts of the Coroner's Court walls were covered in Victorian wooden panelling; the workmen accidentally burnt parts of them black with their blowtorches. Shortly after this I was in my office when the Coroner himself, Dr Gordon Davies, made a rare appearance, bursting into the mortuary in a fury.

'What's wrong?' I asked.

'These morons have removed my lamp from the court!'

Sure enough, Dr Davies' antique brass lamp, which had worked perfectly for more than 50 years had been chucked and replaced with a cheap plastic lamp, which was designed to look like antique brass (but was in fact nothing like it). I, along with various court staff, climbed into the skips and searched until we found the original, which was immediately placed back on Dr Davies' desk.

Eight weeks later, the council declared us fit for business. Our first PM was a gruesome case featuring a six-week-old baby. A commuter on an early morning train arriving at London Bridge Station had seen a young mother stuffing tissue paper into her baby's mouth and called for help as she got off the train. An off-duty police officer had grabbed the baby and ran with it the short distance to Guy's casualty, where it was pronounced dead on arrival.

However, with the baby on the table, we were soon surrounded by ankle-deep water. We tried to carry on with the PM of the baby, but the floor was as slippery as polished steel covered in grease. Professor Johnson slipped and kicked a tray of dissecting tools into the air, causing us all to duck. I called Dr West while Professor Johnson stormed off, soaking wet, to find a change of clothes. The builders had somehow managed to mess up the laying of the epoxy-resin so that groundwater could bubble up through it. The mortuary was closed once more and the floor was relaid, but after reopening, when we placed the body of a murder victim (a woman stabbed 86 times in broad daylight; the murderer was never caught) on the ground for photos, the body fluids reacted with the resin, staining the floor so badly that it had to be relaid a third time.

New lighting had been installed, but it was so dim that I was forced to run out to a lighting store with Pat to purchase a set of six stand-alone lamps so that we could at least see the operating area. The heating system was also a disaster in that it failed to heat. We had to dash out again, this time for Calor gas heaters. However, all this paled into insignificance when it came to the expensive ventilation system.

We were supposed to have eight air changes an hour; the new unit only provided four. Therefore, the serious problem of bad odours seeping into the Coroner's Court was even worse. The council tried to pretend as though these were all 'teething troubles'; after all, the project had cost hundreds of thousands of pounds and they didn't want to have to face tough questioning from the Council's Chief Executive and the Borough Councillors. I submitted report after report to my bosses, but nothing changed because they didn't want to alert anyone else to their incompetence.

In the meantime, we had to open and get back up to full operating capacity. London had never seen a busier time in terms of unexplained and suspicious deaths, and our colleagues in other London mortuaries were struggling to cope with our caseload. We had to crack on, even if it meant enduring foul air in cold and damp rooms. We were immediately asked to take on bodies from Lambeth and Wandsworth, much smaller mortuaries that had become overwhelmed with death as we plunged into deepest winter. It didn't help us that such requests from other boroughs were encouraged by Southwark because we were paid a substantial fee for each body we accepted.

THE STRESS WAS starting to get to me. I was constantly irritable through lack of sleep, and lack of support from the council. At the same time, I was completely addicted to the job and I allowed nothing to interfere with my duty, and that included my family.

Days after reopening, I barely had time to place my head on the pillow before I was summoned out to attend the scene of a drowned man in Dulwich Park with Professor Johnson. The detective at the scene at first thought it might have been murder, but the man was naked and a torchlight search of the area around the pond led us to a pile of neatly folded clothes by a fence. Professor Johnson concluded it was unlikely a murderer had folded the victim's clothes and so confirmed the likely cause as suicide, for reasons unknown.

Bright and early the following morning, the bedroom door flew open and my excited four-year-old son leapt onto my bed, laughing with delight.

'For goodness sake, what are you doing!?' I yelled. 'Get out!'

When I emerged some time later, bags under my eyes, crumpled pyjamas, hair sticking up, looking like I'd been caught in a tornado, I was confronted with the sight of a tear-ful son sitting at the dining table next to a card and present. It took me a few more seconds to register: it was my birthday!

What I didn't know was that Wendy had spent the last few days teaching our son to sing happy birthday to his father. My heart broke at that moment. This was unforgivable, something I could never, ever take back. My poor son had seen a terrible side to his father.

AT WORK THAT day I was met with another bizarre request from the council. The overtime bills of mortuary staff were high thanks to the sheer number of out-of-hours forensic PMs. In cases that were urgent, the pathologist would phone and request that I come directly to the mortuary, no matter what time it was. The very nature of the cases, i.e. murders that needed urgent investigation, dictated that we operated 24-7.

Pathologists even preferred doing some PMs out of office hours, simply because their typical working day was full to the brim. Each morning would be spent dealing with deaths from natural causes and giving evidence in the Coroner's Court. A hurried lunch would be followed by report writing and making sure the relevant samples were sent off to the lab before going on to Crown Courts to give evidence in murder trials. At some point there would be lectures to deliver to medical students, followed by correspondence and research, usually performed in the evening (murders permitting). It was little wonder they wanted to deal with murder cases straight away if they came up out of office hours, and this suited the police just fine.

The council had decided that this had to end as they'd spent so much of their budget on the renovations. I was ordered to confine all murder case PMs to Monday to Friday between the hours of 8am and 4pm. Should a murder occur at midnight on Friday, I was to tell the murder squad to come back on Monday morning!

Apart from the obvious delay this would cause to an urgent investigation, possibly allowing a suspect to escape the country, there were countless other problems to consider, such as the decomposition of trace evidence (body fluids, for example), while increasing the chances of cross-contamination (and even if not, a skilled barrister would be able to free their client based on a delayed PM, claiming cross-contamination and evidential decay would have inevitably occurred over an extended period).

I met with the Coroner Dr Davies and a DI from Scotland Yard to discuss the issue. The DI came up with a simple but effective solution.

'Peter Everett, I am arresting you for obstructing the police in the course of our duties.'

'Excuse me?' I said.

'Come on, Peter, you're nicked; there's a nice cuppa waiting for you down the Yard. And if the council doesn't see sense after that, I'll nick Professor Johnson next.'

'Good luck with that,' I said, getting up.

I used my one phone call to call the council. Seeing the error of their ways, they relented and I was 'released'.

WINTER SEEMED TO drag on that year, a sign of a hot summer to come, perhaps, but for now at least, the days were brutal, and the elderly were dropping in droves. The fridges held 48 bodies, but we ran out of space and often bodies had to be piled up on top of each other on the floor. As much as I believed that the body was just a vessel, the sight of those freshly vacated vessels lying atop one another was just appalling. At one point we ended up with 75 bodies at once, and, thanks to the disastrous renovations, the conditions in which they were kept and in which PMs were performed (dark and damp) were Dickensian to say the least.

It didn't help that Lurch, our porter/cleaner, actually made things worse and Sally and I wasted precious time cleaning up after him. Whenever Lurch did offer to clean something, if Sally or myself were in earshot, we rushed to stop him and give him some other chore. I wanted to fire him but I had no one lined up to replace him, let alone any time to conduct interviews. At least he was capable of wheeling bodies from A to B.

The pathologists, as temperamental as a box of frogs at the best of times, found these conditions intolerable, not least because they ended up bashing elbows with their colleagues (aka rivals) as multiple PMs took place simultaneously in overcrowded conditions.

Professor Johnson almost flipped when he found himself knocking elbows with Professor James 'Taffy' Cameron. Unlike Professor Johnson, everyone liked Professor Cameron. Taffy was kind and patient with his students, and his expertise had been called upon by police forces from around the world. He had performed the PM of Rudolf Hess, former deputy Führer to Adolf Hitler, who hung himself aged 93 while in Spandau Prison, serving his life sentence for 'crimes against peace'. Taffy, a great eccentric, was also famous for having found a box in his office containing original exhibits from the case of Jack the Ripper. He had been using the box as a footrest for years before he decided to take a look inside.

The reason why Professor Johnson hated poor Taffy so much was mainly because Taffy was the rival who had been chosen over him to take the role of Chair of Forensic Medicine at the London Hospital.

It was clear to me that if I didn't want to have to endure the extended rantings and ravings of Professor Johnson, I was going to have to go back to the council and explain what a mess the mortuary was now in. To my relief, further renovations were ordered. This time I was consulted, and so I requested some modifications that would make the building user-friendly. This included a larger and brighter viewing gallery for the murder squad, as well as some much-needed extra fridge space.

My joy was short lived, however. My viewing gallery was an absolute disaster. The builders had decided that an un-tiled breezeblock wall would be fine, making the room a pathogenic nightmare. All these problems stemmed from the fact that we simply had too many senior executives on the council and not enough money. No one at the council had any experience in running a mortuary, and none of them came to visit the building for fear of seeing a dead body.

We needed more money but the council said they simply didn't have it. So I took the thermonuclear option and threatened to resign, enclosing a report detailing the risk to public health from infection and to criminal cases from contamination along with a couple of photographs. I explained that copies of the report would be sent to the press. To my relief, my bluff worked, the council refused to accept my resignation and, miraculously, we suddenly had enough money to do all that we needed. With a superhuman effort made by builders, pathologists and assistants, and with the cooperation of mortuary managers across the capital, this time they did it right – or at least they did until …

I WAS HALTED one morning at the mortuary's front door by one of the foremen. He was a decent enough man and, like myself, had a great many struggles with the council, trying to carry out a difficult job under trying circumstances.

Fed up with the sight of his miserable face, however, I couldn't help but snap 'What now?' but forgot my annoyance the next moment when I saw that he was holding a human skull.

'Where the hell did this come from?' I demanded.

'Just outside your front door, under the step.' I took the skull and, after consulting the records office, recalled that the mortuary had been built over Marshalsea Prison's cemetery. After consultation with the council, we decided not to pursue the matter; we simply couldn't afford any more disruption.

A few days later, Professor Johnson and I arrived at work together early one morning as he had a suspicious death to examine before dashing off to the Old Bailey, where he was due to give evidence in a murder case.

'I don't know, Peter,' he sighed, stamping irritably around the PM room while Pat wheeled in the body. 'All this stress will be the death of me!'

I shrugged and tried to say something sympathetic. Although the building was still in a bit of mess, we were through the worst of it now. Besides, Professor Johnson was always making extreme statements like this.

A couple of hours after the prof had left for the Old Bailey, while Pat was tidying up, I received a phone call from an administrator from Guy's Hospital.

'I'm calling to alert you to the fact that Professor Johnson is no longer able to complete his duties. You'll need to find someone else for any urgent cases that are waiting for him today.'

'What on earth are you talking about?' I asked between puffs on my pipe. 'He was here just a couple of hours ago.'

'I'm afraid Professor Johnson suddenly collapsed and died at the Old Bailey.'

'What? It can't be!'

'I'm afraid so. I'm sorry. His body's already in St Barts' mortuary.'

At first, in shock, I protested that this timeframe couldn't work but, as the clerk reminded me, the Old Bailey was just five minutes' drive away while St Bartholomew's Hospital was just across the road from the famous courthouse.

I was lost for words. My pipe slipped from my fingers and clattered on the floor.

Later that day, a PM found that Professor Johnson had died of a massive heart attack. Regardless of his abrupt manner, we were all stunned by the news. He may have been difficult to work with, but his skills as a pathologist were second to none, and he was always generous with his time. Although Professor Johnson existed in a state of permanent roiling anger, I had come to rely on him as both a colleague and a friend. The world of forensic medicine had lost a great mind. As Shakespeare's Hamlet says: 'He was a man, take him for all in all. I shall not look upon his like again.'

This should have been a clear warning to me about the consequences of stress, but I barely ever seemed to have time to think. The cases came thick and fast, and the longer I spent at Southwark Mortuary, the greater my responsibilities seemed to become. Shortly after Professor Johnson's death we received a body that threw the whole borough into turmoil: the suspicious death of a man with AIDS. This took place at the beginning of the year of so-called AIDS hysteria, when no guidelines specific to the treatment of people with this dreadful illness existed – except to treat the poor souls as though they had a plague that could leap between bodies with a single look. MP and Junior Health Secretary Edwina Currie hadn't helped by announcing that 'good Christians won't get AIDS'. The council ordered us not to open the body for fear of infection. Fortunately, we only needed a toxicology report, so I took fluid from the eye and this proved sufficient.

As Professor Johnson was laid to rest, and as the renovations were finally completed, I reflected that now, with the corruption scandal behind me, with Pat and Sally by my side, and with the support of pathologists like Professor Mant, we might have just about succeeded in dragging the mortuary system into the 20th century. Which was just as well, because in the coming months and years the mortuary was going to be tested as it had never been before.

15

What lies beneath

October 1986

My first blow after the mortuary's restoration came from Pat, who turned in his resignation.

'Are you sure?' I asked.

Pat nodded. A man of few words, he was never one to go back on a decision. I tried to persuade him to stay but Pat was one of life's nomads. He was never able to stay in a job for more than a couple of years before the desire to move on overtook him.

I was devastated. Pat was the one person I completely trusted.

Finding a replacement proved to be an impossible task. No one wanted to become deputy to the man who had cost just about everyone in the mortuary service a fortune in back taxes. And, despite my best efforts, Southwark's reputation for dodgy goings-on persisted.

I was desperate, so took desperate measures. A young lady called Mary had joined us as a mortuary technician on a voluntary basis. She had passed her training and so I decided – although this was exceedingly early in her career – that she would make a reasonable deputy.

No one who met Mary ever forgot her. She was beautiful, and before joining Southwark Mortuary she had worked as a model, frequently appearing in glossy magazines, wearing anything from swimsuits to evening wear. I didn't know why she had been drawn to work in the mortuary (she did joke that at least the dead didn't try to grope her), although, as events would prove, I think the mortuary, at this time at least, seemed to attract unusual characters.

At the time, the only thing I could classify as odd about her was her propensity for bad language (she could out-curse even the most foul-mouthed detectives) and her habit of chain smoking. Besides that, everyone had good things to say about her (often where the men were concerned, with faraway looks in their eyes). Mary had also given us a bonus in bringing along Marjorie, her mother, whom everyone loved. 'Marj', a true cockney, worked in the Coroner's Court as a cleaner, but she also enjoyed acting as our unofficial tea lady. I'd be discussing a case in the PM room with the murder squad only to be interrupted by Marj, armed with tea and cake and a raft of cheeky jokes, and suddenly it felt as though we were guests in her home.

WITH ONE PROBLEM solved, another remained: Lurch the

cleaner. I hadn't realised quite how much Pat had done to cover Lurch's inadequacies. I came down one afternoon to find the mortuary's floors streaked with pink smears. Checking the fridges, I discovered that they'd developed a stink that was, upon opening the doors, like being slapped in the face with a rotten fish. Previously, Pat had kept the mortuary spotless with a daily two-hour cleaning programme. It now took Lurch six hours and it was still dirty, as was he, for his personal hygiene was also worthy of some concern. If this wasn't enough, I also started receiving a number of complaints from funeral directors who had been presented with unwashed bodies. Even worse, one funeral director arrived at the mortuary to return a body that Lurch had released to him by mistake. I handed over the correct one, apologising profusely.

I submitted reports to my immediate boss, but each time I received the same reply: 'Enter the details in the day book.' Lurch had received three verbal warnings but, according to council rules, he needed three written warnings for the situation to be taken seriously and my boss, not wanting to reveal the poor state the mortuary was in and therefore his poor management, didn't pass on my reports. I was stuck, for the moment at least.

This meant I had to clean up after Lurch at the end of the day, with Mary's help, if I could persuade her, which wasn't often. Since her promotion, Mary had started coming in late and leaving early, citing the not unreasonable excuse that she had a young son to look after, but this was something she had failed to mention during our interview. This state of affairs meant I regularly had to work late into the night, cleaning and carrying out administration tasks. Meanwhile, Professor Mant and Dr West complained that, thanks to Lurch's laziness and Mary's absences, they kept arriving to find that bodies weren't prepped for their PMs and that no one was around to assist them.

The stress played havoc with my family life; on those rare occasions when I was home when Wendy and my son were awake, I was fatigued and extremely irritable. I never took sick days and regarded those who did with suspicion (i.e., Lurch) but, what with Wendy's exasperation at my exhaustion, I agreed to take a few days' annual leave and let Mary captain the ship. Upon my return to the mortuary I was informed that a ring had gone missing from one of the bodies.

Mix-ups did happen. Sometimes there might be four bodies arriving and two being released and, once in a blue moon, someone would place an item with the wrong body. But, after going over the admissions system with the coroners and the staff on the reception desk, I realised that something far more sinister might have taken place.

After items were removed from a body, they were listed in a notebook, wrapped in plastic bags and then placed in a drawer in the mortuary reception desk until all the other admissions were complete. Then they were placed in the safe, which I soon discovered wasn't the safest place. Regulations stated that only coroner's officers should have access to the safe, but if they were 'busy', they left the keys in reception so that whoever happened to be on duty could return items to grieving relatives without delay. This slap-dash approach had either led to the ring's loss, or, as much as I dreaded to even consider the possibility, we had a new thief in the mortuary.

Shortly after the missing ring incident, my boss invited me out for a coffee. At first I was pleased. I thought that he'd realised at long last that we need to take some urgent steps to sort the mortuary out. Instead, he handed me a written warning. While I'd been on leave he'd paid a rare visit to the mortuary and found the keys to the safe lying on a desk. The responsibility had been Mary's because I was a hundred miles away, and yet it was I who received the written warning. And still he didn't listen to my urgent requests for help. The reason I was making mistakes, that the mortuary ship wasn't as watertight as it could be, was because its captain was on the verge of a nervous breakdown. Taking a break had only led to more trouble. I was speeding towards collapse but felt too paralysed to do anything about it.

News of my written warning soon spread. Lurch had already taken great delight in the fact that I couldn't fire him, and now he knew that my boss didn't like me. So, he upped his insubordination by taking even more sick days. It became the case that I was often the only person on duty. I had to eviscerate bodies, attend PMs, reconstitute the bodies and clean the mortuary by myself. This was in addition to report writing, answering just about every phone call on every subject that came through the mortuary, as well as dealing with funeral directors and murder detectives.

A shake-up in the police force had resulted in new coroner's officers working at the mortuary, but once these new constables realised they had no one to report to, i.e. there was no ranking police officer, they decided to take it easy. They got all their paperwork done in the morning and then, come lunchtime, their office turned into the Casino Royale. Whiskey would flow as they played poker for cash beneath thick clouds of cigarette smoke.

The following week, after giving my quarterly lecture on forensic PMs to the London Fire Brigade's training school, I returned to the mortuary to find Mary in tears while Brian the coroner's officer was, unusually for him, mopping the floor (albeit slowly) while frowning and mumbling to himself. A pathologist had had his wallet stolen while working on a murder case in the mortuary. The thief had struck with the murder squad just a few metres away, and the detective superintendent had asked Mary and Lurch if he could search them so as to eliminate them from suspicion. Following protocol, he should have called in a female police constable to search Mary, but as the team had worked together for some time no objections were made. Nothing was found on either of them and it was assumed that an opportunist thief had snuck through the unlocked mortuary door. However, shortly after the search, Mary got in touch with her union, claiming that she had been assaulted by the officer.

By all other accounts, including Lurch's, the police officers' and the pathologists', the detective superintendent had simply checked her pockets; nothing like a pat down or strip search had taken place. Nevertheless, the following day Mary's union contact threatened strike action. Crisis talks were held at head office. Matters were exacerbated with the arrival of a senior officer from Scotland Yard. More statements were taken, and the detective superintendent who had ordered and carried out the search faced suspension. He was eventually cleared and escaped punishment, but the victim of the theft did not. The pathologist was blamed for reporting the theft to those police officers who happened to be present instead of going through the proper channels (whatever they were). The union, in its wisdom, decided to ban the unfortunate pathologist from working in Southwark Mortuary for six weeks.

OF COURSE, DEATH went on. I was in my cold and draughty office, working my way through a deep pile of paperwork, when the phone rang. Thousands of skeletons had been found under Guy's Hospital and I had been appointed exhumations officer.

London is a city built on bones. A succession of Romans, Saxons, Normans, Tudors, Georgians, Regents and Victorians have each added a layer to an archaeological cake about ten metres deep. Their remains are today covered by some of London's most famous landmarks, including St Paul's Cathedral. Sir Christopher Wren cared little about the Roman ruins discovered when digging the foundations, but fortunately for us a local antiquarian by the name of John Conyers did. Conyers took notes and extracted pot fragments, bones and other artefacts in what is now regarded as one of the world's first archaeological investigations. Ever since then, London archaeology has become a crucial part of the city's constant redevelopment. The more we build, the more we learn about our city and the people who lived here before us.

Up until my phone call, London's two largest burial grounds were thought to be one close to Liverpool Street Station, the so-called 'New Churchyard' (London's first municipal cemetery, dating back to the Middle Ages), and Bedlam's burial grounds (this was the name by which Bethlem Royal Hospital was known, London's first psychiatric hospital). Together, these hosted the bodies of up to 25,000 Londoners. Many were victims of the Great Plague of 1665 which killed about 100,000 people – one in five Londoners.

As it turned out, the discovery at Guy's Hospital, on the building site of a new tower block, would lead to the exhumation of 21,000 bodies. After obtaining an exhumation license from the Home Office, I was put in touch with the Museum of London's Archaeology (MOLA) department. Together we came up with a plan to recover the bodies and have them re-interred at the 68-acre Camberwell New Cemetery in the suburbs of South East London, which had plenty of room and then some. The owners of Camberwell New Cemetery, no doubt realising that death was a growth industry, had bought swathes of land at rock-bottom prices in the early 20th century, but faced stiff competition from other private cemeteries and so had never come close to filling the space.

The Home Office's exhumation licence stipulated that the working area had to be secure and out of public view. Security wasn't a problem, but after travelling to the site, I could see that keeping the exhumations out of sight was going to be tricky. The entire area was overlooked by the main hospital building, which meant that patients would have a bird's-eye view of archaeologists digging up skeletons. I eventually found a company that was able to construct and install high canvas screens around the immediate work area which were angled in such a way that obscured the view from everything but pigeons.

The work was slow. Fortunately, because I was so close by and because I only needed to check the site once a day, I was able to carry on with my duties at the mortuary as it progressed. I had precious little time as it was for overseeing what was then London's largest archaeological dig, which was taking place at the great displeasure of the contractors. Finds like these are an expensive headache for the businesses concerned for two reasons: firstly, all building work has to stop until the dig is done. Secondly, the contractors must pay for all the archaeological work.

On the flip side, MOLA's osteologists (bone specialists) were in their element. For them, every day of the six months of the dig was a field day. Surrounded by diggers that could move tonnes of earth in a few minutes, they attacked the damp, clay-like soil with spoons and brushes, exposing skeleton after skeleton, every bone of which was recorded on a log sheet. Any valuables, such as rings or religious artefacts were also logged and removed to one of the Museum of London's specialist storage facilities.

After a few weeks, we learned that there were three burial areas, all from the Georgian period (1714–1830). The outer ring was for the poorest (the bodies were tightly packed with no headstones), the next for the middle classes (more widely spaced with the occasional statue) and finally, behind the remains of tall iron railings, was the 'inner sanctum', a closed-off area in which the upper classes had been entombed.

I happened to be present the day that one of the largest tombs was opened. It was about the size of a gatekeeper's cottage, roomy enough for a large family. Inside was a large wooden coffin, covered in ornamental brass work. When the coffin was opened, we gazed down upon the body of a perfectly-preserved army general in full dress uniform, complete with sword and medals. He was in such good condition that for a moment I wondered if someone was pulling my leg and he was about to sit up and point at me, and everyone would fall about laughing at my expense. As one of the osteologists explained, however, the famous London damp preserved fabric, leather, wood and metal that in drier cities would rot and rust away.

The bones were subjected to detailed analysis in MOLA's lab, and this served to highlight how tough people had it in Georgian times. Apart from the fact that *everyone*, without exception, suffered from terrible dental problems, particularly abscesses, the analyses revealed high levels of malnutrition, as well as warped backs and limbs (the result of intense physical labour), chronic infections (predominantly syphilis) and violence (from the number of people whose skulls had been cracked by a blunt instrument or bones that bore the marks of a blade passing through their body). Most surprising, perhaps, was the high number of children – about 40 per cent – reflecting the incredibly high infant mortality rates. By the time the exhumations were complete, over 21,000 skeletons had been re-interred, and the Museum of London had acquired hundreds of new artefacts.

A few weeks later, I received a call from an environmental health officer about another discovery. Builders excavating the ground below one of the countless Victorian railway arches near London Bridge had been shocked to uncover a row of human skulls. After some careful archaeological work, it was revealed that these skeletons – 200 of them – had been buried vertically. None had coffins or shrouds. There were no headstones or relics. MOLA's osteologists were stumped. Although some of the bones had markings on them which suggested that they'd been through a PM, there were no records of a graveyard of any sort ever having been in the area. Carbon dating suggested the burial took place at some point in the early 1700s, ruling out the Black Death. This find still remains one of London's many historical mysteries.

These sorts of events always seem to come in threes and, sure enough, a few weeks after the London Bridge case I was called to attend a church in Bermondsey after police had received reports that children had been using a human skull as a football. The site of this macabre match was the grounds of St George's Church in Wells Way. One of the many Waterloo churches built in 1824 to celebrate the Duke of Wellington's 1815 victory over Napoleon at Waterloo, St George's had seen better days. In its prime it had stood as a towering landmark in what was otherwise open park-land but now, shadowed by a block of council flats, it was nothing but a Grade II-listed ruin. A fire had claimed the roof and the crumbling walls were covered in graffiti. On top of this, an expressive bronze statue of Christ – one of the countless memorials to the fallen of the First World War commissioned in 1919 – had been stolen. The church's owners – the Nigerian Celestial Church of Christ – had just made a public appeal for its return. As I investigated the ruins, picking my way carefully through the interior, which was now overgrown with young trees, weeds and blackberry bushes, I stumbled across a hole in the wall, large enough to clamber through. The crypt. Luckily, I had brought my murder bag, which contained a torch. Working my way cautiously inside, I stepped into a truly bizarre and most macabre scene. The crypt was full of coffins, some of which had been broken into. A stake had been rammed into the chest of the body of one unfortunate inhabitant, and many other bodies were missing, including those of two children. As I made my way deeper into the crypt, I passed through a narrower tunnel that led to the private family vaults of Victorian gentry. These had been protected from looters by wrought iron bars. A faded brass plate identified one owner as 'Arthur Rolls, Esq., of Manor Place', whose coffin was covered in dark blue felt.

Overall, I counted 137 coffins, nineteen of which had been forced open. Most worryingly, from an environmental health point of view, was that two of the most recently opened coffins were still full of blood. Thanks to the lead-lined oak coffins and the damp air, fluids had been preserved, and this meant that it was possible that Victorian bacteria and diseases may have also been preserved, perhaps even smallpox.

I swung my torch around and nearly dropped it in surprise when I spotted something decidedly un-Victorian: opened cans of baked beans, blankets, matches, cigarette ends and evidence of a recent fire. Vagrants were living down here. Now that *was* a cause for concern – if any viruses had survived, these people had a real risk of catching them.

I immediately contacted environmental health and the borough's engineering department, who came and sealed the crypt straight away. I recommended that the church be demolished, and the rubble used to fill in the crypt so there would never be any chance of disease spreading.

Things turned out rather differently. The sealed coffins, including Arthur Rolls, Esq., were removed and buried at Nunhead Cemetery while the opened ones were destroyed. Shortly after this, the Celestial Church of Christ found a buyer for the church, and today it's owned by a housing association who converted the building into a number of one-bedroom apartments. Even the bronze statue of Christ has been returned to its rightful place after it was discovered in a Brixton scrapyard.

SPECTACULAR DISCOVERIES ARE still waiting to be made. Just about every major building project in recent years has unearthed something of crucial importance: Neolithic, Roman and Saxon settlements below Heathrow's Terminal 5; a 6,000-year-old port next to the MI6 building in Vauxhall; and an ancient temple built in 240 AD in honour of the Roman god Mithras, god of the sun and justice, at Bloomberg's new

European headquarters in the City of London. Archaeologists dubbed this site the 'Pompeii of the North' thanks to the extraordinary condition of recovered coins, amulets, pewter plates, ceramic lamps, 250 leather boots and sandals, and more than 900 boxes of pottery. Meanwhile, in Liverpool Street archaeologists have sifted their way down to the early Roman level where they discovered human remains stored in old cooking pots which sat alongside 40 human skulls, possibly the results of a mass execution.

Other graves have been found in Stratford, East London, when the Olympic Park was being built (going back to Neolithic times) and in Covent Garden when an extension was added to the Royal Opera House (the body of a noble Saxon woman). At the moment, all the excitement is centred on the multi-billion-pound Crossrail project, the east–west London underground commuter rail link that is both Europe's largest engineering project and its biggest archaeological dig. People wonder why it's running late. Well, just about every time the rotors turn on the huge tunnel ten metres below London, archaeologists are watching, waiting to pounce. The total number and type of discoveries, macabre and otherwise, has yet to be announced, but we do know that the discoveries made so far span 70,000 years, a healthy reminder that all of us are playing small parts in an enormous, never-ending story.

16

The accidental pathologist

November 1986

Professor Mant groaned. We were in the foul room, a man's badly decomposed body before us. He'd been found in a flat in the North Peckham council estate when the downstairs neighbours had called the police after maggots had found their way into the floor and dropped through the ceiling onto their bed below.

However, Professor Mant hadn't groaned because of the stink.

'My back!' he exclaimed, doubling over. 'I just can't manage another.'

It had been a typically busy morning in the mortuary with three PMs already done. I told the prof to take a seat while I washed some of the maggots off by hosing the body down with warm water.

As he did so, he sighed. 'You'll have to do it, Peter. I'll supervise from here. You'll be fine,' he added seeing my uncertainty. 'I'm going to have a quick lie down and stretch out in the relatives' room. You can fetch me in when the body's prepped and on the table.'

I was honoured but exhausted and wondered how much longer I could continue myself. I couldn't remember the last time I hadn't felt exhausted. Each night, I went through the same routine, staggering through the front door and, if I was able, stopping for a few mouthfuls of food – barely having the energy to eat, let alone to tell Wendy about my day (after all, I hardly wanted to go through it all again and I preferred to spare her the details anyway) – before collapsing into bed. Upon the alarm's ring the following morning (if I was lucky enough to sleep through the night undisturbed by telephone or young son), I didn't feel as though I'd rested for even a wink. At least I didn't have nightmares – I slept like the dead.

That morning over breakfast, as I stared into a cup of tea as if it were the well of sadness, Wendy had repeated a question, often asked in exasperation: 'For goodness sake, Peter, why don't you resign? You're depressed most of the time, and this job will be the death of you!'

She was right. I was like a zombie at home, and when I could summon up any emotion, it was largely despair, which would come and go in waves. Every few weeks I would rally and tell myself it would be alright, that the nightmare would pass, that this was the result of a busy job with hefty responsibility, mixed with life lived with a young family in the world's greatest city. The nightmare never did pass. At the time, I had no idea what was happening to me or what I was on the verge of if I didn't take drastic action. But, thanks to Wendy, I did understand that the job was the root cause. So, that morning, I took her advice and drafted a resignation letter. I walked the short distance to work, the envelope sitting as heavy as lead in the inside pocket of my suit jacket. Before I could pop my termination into the internal post, however, a murder was already awaiting my attention and, like all murders, there was no time to waste.

It FELT LIKE there was something in the air that summer, and I'm not talking about the nuclear fallout from Chernobyl. The murders came thick and fast, and life in the mortuary became crazier with each passing day. That month we investigated 33 further suspicious deaths, nineteen of which turned out to be murder.

The victim in the first case that morning, identified to Professor Mant and me by DCI David Oakley, was Vahid Atashzai. He arrived at the mortuary bound and gagged. Black tape had been wrapped around his mouth.

'Mr Atashzai worked at the Kentucky Fried Chicken on the Norwood Road,' DCI Oakley explained. 'He was the manager and the staff found him this morning when they arrived for work. The safe's empty.'

We learned that Vahid, 30 years old, slim and handsome, had been born in Iran, where he'd been trained as an electrical engineer. He'd failed to find a job in his chosen field in the UK but found inspiration in his job at KFC, where he was a model employee, sometimes working sixteen-hour days. Everyone he knew heard of his dreams of opening his own restaurant and they all knew it would be a huge success.

'The thieves had broken into the KFC, lain in wait for Mr Atashzai, and ambushed him in the morning,' DCI Oakley continued. 'They tied him up, taking the keys to the safe and making off with, according to the receipt book, £2,000.'

'Looks like the tape's pretty much obstructing his nostrils,' Professor Mant observed. 'So possible asphyxia by smothering, or "burking" as it used to be known.'

In cases of murder, some experts still occasionally referred to smothering as 'burking' after the infamous Burke and Hare murders. At that time (1828), the only legal source of cadavers for medical educators came from the executioner's noose, i.e. executed prisoners. There was such a demand that some doctors paid handsomely, no questions asked, for pretty much any cadaver that was wheeled to their doorstop. Burke and Hare spotted a gap in the market, and, selecting victims from the hopelessly drunk, they suffocated them (this way the corpses had no visible injuries and could be purchased in all 'innocence') and sold them on for up to £10 a time. They managed to sell a dozen cadavers before they were caught, executed and ended up on the dissection table at Edinburgh's medical school.

In some ways we hadn't come very far in more than one and a half centuries. Although the means were different and people weren't being murdered with this sole intention, there was still a black market in body parts. After a post-mortem was complete, some pathologists would agree to brains being given to medical schools for student use. This was perfectly legal at the time (the Human Tissue Act of 2004 ended this practice). However, technicians still sometimes sold body parts, such as brains, eyes and bones, to medical researchers, manufacturers and universities. This was all highly illegal and my exposé of corruption in the mortuary had done little to halt such practices across the UK, as I would later discover.

At the PM, it became apparent that while Vahid had been able to inhale a little air through his nose, it had not been enough to survive and he had slowly suffocated – needless to say, a terrible way to have to die. What should have been a simple case of robbery, thanks to the criminal idiots involved, had become murder. And then there was Vihad's young wife, Bernadette, who arrived at the mortuary with their seven-week-old baby son, Adam. I usually didn't have to make too much of an effort to keep my emotions separate from work, but this was a tough one. The sight of that mother and baby, combined with the trussed-up body we'd photographed lying on the mortuary floor, well, it was enough to make anyone weep.

Perhaps unsurprisingly, considering their inept methods when it came restraint, DCI Oakley's team quickly found the robbers partying away the proceeds. Andrew Chung was in his late teens while Anthony Tull was 21. There was a question for a time as to whether to charge them with murder or manslaughter, but the CPS agreed that, although the robbers were callous, they were also incompetent. Their intention hadn't been to murder their victim, only to prevent him from interfering with their robbery and raising the alarm after they had left. Both men were sentenced to twelve years.

It was a case of déjà vu as the next murder I dealt with also featured a body that had been bound and gagged. This was recently retired road sweeper David Sandall, aged 65. A neighbour had seen David's back door swinging open and, suspecting a burglary, called the police. A constable found David bound and gagged on the first floor landing.

David had taken early retirement the previous year and had received a cash payment of £7,000, so it was possible that the robbers knew about this and had hoped to find some of it at his home. A widower, he'd lived alone in his two-storey maisonette for the last six months or so, ever since his lodger and son had moved out.

Once we removed the cloth from his mouth, we found a sock stuffed inside. It was this which had blocked the flow of air from his nose into his lungs. His wrists and ankles had been bound with electrical flex. The house had been ransacked, but David's money was still safe in his bank account. At first it was thought that the same pair who robbed the KFC might have attacked David as the two addresses were close to one another, but the KFC killers had already been picked up by the time David was murdered and, unfortunately, his killer was never found.

And now we had the stinker to deal with. Maggots were crawling all over it and I blasted as many of them off as I could with the formaldehyde solution.

Mary appeared, cigarette in hand, as I brought the body into the PM room. She was dressed as usual in designer clothes, which I presumed formed part of the proceeds of her modelling career. She couldn't have looked more out of place at that moment.

'Jesus fucking Christ, Peter,' she said, her cockney accent breaking her sophisticated image. 'Ain't we got any fucking air freshener?'

I shook my head. 'Sorry, no. Not that that'd be much help anyway. And the extractor fans have never been that great, so I'm afraid we'll just have to grin and bear it.'

I had to agree that this was utterly awful; the odour was so strong it made you sweat.

The past summer, Mary had taken to sunbathing on the roof with Sally during her lunch break, which had caused a sensation in the mortuary and coroner's court, as just about every able-bodied man tried to make sure they timed their lunch break or extended cigarette break just right, so they would have the chance to gawp. She faced incessant requests for dates and promises of great times to be had, and while she enjoyed joking with the funeral director and coroner's officers, she always cited the fact that she was happily married.

'I've been wanting to apologise to you, Peter,' she continued from a distance, her hand covering her nose. I'd started studying the stinker up close. In cases of decomposition, as the body swells with gas, the soft, rotting flesh separates, causing large holes to appear in the skin. These holes should have pieces of tissue running across them, the result of the way decaying flesh behaves when stretched – a bit like wet glue. I'd been checking that this was the case, for any holes without striations signified a stab wound. I looked up in surprise. I'd already given up on Mary, who was only coming into work one day out of every five, and instead had begun to rely heavily on young Sally.

Was Mary about to promise a change for the better? I gazed at her in hope.

'It's my husband Tom,' she said. 'This isn't easy for me to talk about, you see, but he's in prison.'

'Oh, I'm sorry to hear that.' I replied, unable to think of anything better to say.

'He's always been a bit of a villain,' she continued, 'but he's trying, he really is.'

'I thought he had a full-time job at the meat market.'

'He does, well, did. He was trying to go straight but his friends are a bad influence, you know. And he's violent sometimes. He was inside for eighteen months, for GBH. Me and Jack [her son] live in fear really.'

'Why don't you leave him?'

'It's not that easy. He'd find me anywhere I went. At least with this job, I have some breathing space. But he's coming out soon and I'm scared. You see, I've been having an affair.'

'Oh yes? Anyone I know?'

'Yes, actually you do. It's Ben Clarke.'

My mouth dropped open surprise. 'What, as in DS Ben Clarke from London Bridge?' Ben was a tough but fair 30-something murder-squad detective who was a regular at Southwark, and I was pretty sure he was married. I'd had absolutely no idea. 'Well, you certainly have an interesting life,' I added, still uncertain as to what else to say. 'Thank you for telling me, but do you think you could try and be here a little more often than you have been lately?'

'I will, boss, promise.'

'Great. In that case, would you prep the PM table and then fetch Professor Mant from the relatives' room? I'm going to take a closer look at this fellow.'

As Mary clattered about the place, gathering the various instruments and containers, I bent down to better inspect one of the holes. It sat directly above the heart and there were no strands of flesh stretched across it. Taking a magnifying glass, I examined the cavity and spotted bruises on the surrounding the tissue. A stab wound. I had known the theory but had never witnessed it until then.

Now, as I worked under Professor Mant's direction, performing my first murder post-mortem with my designer-clad assistant, I realised that I was desperately needed. In fact, I realised, no one qualified would even want this job, thanks to the mortuary's bad reputation. Professor Mant wouldn't be able to ask anyone else to help him at times when his back gave out because he didn't trust anyone as much as he trusted me.

The mortuary needed me.

The dead needed me.

I walked home with the unsent resignation letter in my jacket pocket.

'What else am I going to do?' I said to an exasperated Wendy. 'No other mortuary would have me for a start, and I don't know how to do anything else. We'll lose this flat and we won't be able to pay the rent without regular income. I have to stay and just hope things will get better.'

17

The problem with Peckham

December 1986

Dawn in Peckham is not normally a sight to stir the soul and today was no exception. Added to the grey concrete grimness of the North Peckham Estate, with its dark stairwells and unlit passageways, the badly-spelled graffiti, the overflowing industrial-sized bins, the unpleasant odours and a lack of green space, was the sight of a detective constable vomiting into some spindly bushes that were struggling to grow close to the entranceway of a block of five-storey flats.

Professor Mant and I regularly attended scenes within the so-called Bermondsey Triangle which runs from London Bridge to Peckham and back up the Old Kent Road into Bermondsey. It's named after the Bermuda Triangle thanks to the high incidence of unexplained losses of goods and people within its borders.

Historically, crime is to Southwark what politics are to Westminster. This area has been known for its criminality ever since Henry VIII outlawed prostitution in 1546, forcing Southwark's 16th-century sex industry into the back streets. Indeed, ever since then, the boroughs of Southwark and Lambeth have been seen as North London's disreputable accessory, where all the nasty criminal effluvium could be discharged and left to fester. By the time the Victorian era arrived, South London was home to the stink industries: the tanneries, the glue factories, rubbish dumps, lunatic asylums and prisons, and, naturally enough, crime.

Southwark remains a 'challenging' borough to this day for the Metropolitan Police, but in the 1980s it was like the Wild West. As Radio 4 pundit Arthur Smith once said: 'Up in North London we have blue plaques to commemorate where famous people lived. Down in South London they instead have those yellow boards – you know, murder, stabbing, rape, appeal for witnesses, that kind of thing.'

Most often, perhaps, I was called to attend murder scenes at the North Peckham Estate and its environs. The North Peckham Estate was one of the most deprived residential areas in Western Europe. The largest of Peckham's five council estates, it consisted of 65 five-storey blocks over 40 acres, comprising almost 1,500 homes. When it was built in the mid-1960s, it was hailed as a vision of the future, a first-class example of 'streets in the sky'; a cost efficient use of space that provided an ideal living environment for London's poor. Of course, that vision remained firmly in the dreams of architects and planners and, by the 1980s, residents were commonly subjected to arson attacks, burglaries, robberies and muggings. In just one week in 1987, the police recorded 70 muggings.

At this time unemployment in Peckham was at 31 per cent (London's highest), but for sixteen to nineteen year olds, it had reached the giddy heights of 62 per cent. As local Labour Councillor Mary Ellery put it: 'Unemployment knocked six kinds of shit out of people. Careers officers came into schools with the bad news when kids were fourteen, and from then on they knew there was no bloody point. All you need to know is how to write your name and how to go on the dole. If you're 40-plus, you're on the shit-heap.'

In this context, burglary, where you could make a few hundred pounds each week (a labourer or shop worker might make £40 or £50 a week) was a tempting proposition, as was bank or cash-in-transit robbery. Then there was the relatively new trade of dealing Class A drugs, which was where real fortunes could be made. Apart from marijuana, amphetamines and heroin, a cheap and highly addictive new drug called 'crack' also started to arrive in the UK in the mid-1980s. As residents on the North Peckham Estate who were able to found ways to leave, squatters (often drug dealers) moved in. Addiction to crack soon followed and, needing a phenomenal amount of cash to feed their daily habit (a crack addict might spend anything from £100 to £300 a day), addicts turned to thieving and mugging.

The council's response to rising crime was to add bars to ground floor windows and to provide residents with reinforced front doors. Such measures may have helped prevent burglaries, but they also made the place look even more foreboding and, in some cases, helped crack dealers fortify their dens. By the mid-1980s, many tenants believed that complete demolition was the only answer but, what with 24,000 people on Southwark's waiting list for housing, this was deemed impossible, not forgetting of course that the council was almost broke at the time (it couldn't even afford to evict squatters). In 1979, Southwark's budget to maintain 36,000 homes was £60 million. In the 1980s, Prime Minister Margaret Thatcher launched a programme of austerity which slashed Southwark's budget to £28 million. On top of this, thanks to Mrs T's abolition of the Greater London Council, Southwark had an extra 26,000 properties to care for.

WE WERE MET by DCS Melvin and together we climbed the perpetually dark stairwell (the lifts weren't working) to the third floor and stopped at the first flat on the left. A handful of residents were on the walkways, watching us with annoyed expressions; the crime scene was blocking the only way in and out of their homes.

'Neighbours called us after they saw the door kicked in,' Melvin said, lighting a cigarette. 'It had been pushed closed but was sitting at an odd angle. The PCs thought it was another burglary. The body's in the bathroom. It's not pretty.'

'We'd guessed as much from your colleague's reaction,' Professor Mant said.

He led the way and, as I followed, I noticed that the kitchen, on our left, was bare, save for what looked like some drug paraphernalia on the table: electronic scales, a knife, cling film, along with a few coins scattered on the floor. The only signs of food were a few takeaway boxes, no doubt the victim's last meal. As we moved down the hallway, I saw smears of blood on the wall. The carpeted floor was stained and filthy. The lounge was next. Dark and dirty, with a strong odour of damp and rotting carpet, I could see beer cans on the floor as well as more drug paraphernalia lying on a make-shift table: a pallet with a half a door lying on top.

'Not much sympathy for this one on the estate,' Melvin continued as he led us up the stairs. 'Known drug dealer. Seems like he helped get a lot of people addicted to crack. Local residents were terrified of him.' He stepped aside as we reached the door to the bathroom.

The room was small, just under two metres wide and just over two metres long. I could see the victim's hand hanging over the edge of the bath in which he was lying. As I craned to see over Professor Mant's shoulder, I saw that the water was pink with blood but not completely opaque. Two small pink and white orbs floated on the surface between the man's legs. The victim's testes, cut free of his scrotum. Professor Mant struggled to bend, leaning awkwardly on the side of the bath.

'Mind if I let out the water?' he asked.

'By all means.'

As the pink water drained away, the man's injuries became clear.

'He's been stabbed repeatedly in the heart area,' Professor Mant said. 'No question that the killer wanted to murder him. Judging by the amount of blood, I'd say he was castrated post-mortem.'

'We're thinking rival dealer,' Melvin said. 'The trade in crack is booming right now. This guy's Jamaican, already on the run from the cops back home. Their greatest danger is not us, it's rivals. I've never seen anything like it – they shoot, stab and beat one another to death without a second thought.'

The murder victim had been a yardie, already on the run from police in the US and Jamaica. They'd started arriving in the UK in droves, ready to make some serious drug money on the UK's virgin crack shores. Jamaica was a stopping off point for South American cocaine being smuggled to North America and into Europe and, with the emergence of crack, which is easy to make, addictive and cheaper than other Class A drugs, the yardies, with plenty of family connections to the UK, had seen a way to get rich quick. They also loved the fact that the UK cops didn't carry guns.

As Professor Mant completed his examination, I sketched the scene and took some measurements. The case looked straightforward enough from our perspective, but Melvin was going to have his work cut out catching the murderer.

'Removing the man's balls was a clear warning,' he said as a uniformed officer started to remove the crime scene tape so residents could walk by. 'Anyone crosses this guy then he's coming at them in the most savage way possible. Finding witnesses, let alone anyone prepared to give evidence, is going to be an uphill battle.'

We wished him luck and took our leave. As we descended the stairs we passed a young woman on the second floor landing. She had a pram and a toddler.

'You couldn't give me hand, could you?' she asked. 'Lift's buggered yet again.'

Excusing Professor Mant's bad back, I took one end of the pram and helped the young lady carry it down.

'Used to be a nice place this,' she said. 'I mean, it was always a bit rough around the edges, but over the last couple of years or so, it's turned into a nightmare. Needles in the corridor. Kids peeing in the stairwells. Stealing and mugging. I've had to step over junkies, passed out on these stairs before.'

I noted the acrid smell of stale urine and high-strength lager while looking into the eyes of the innocent young toddler sitting in the pram before me. What kind of place was this to raise a child? What future lay in wait for him? It also struck me that Wendy and I were raising our own son, who was a similar age, not ten minutes' drive away.

I started to feel anxiety rise within me. I didn't know it, of course, but I was drawing close to my breaking point. Shortly after seeing that toddler in the pushchair, I'd felt something snap inside me, like another crack in a dam that would eventually burst, and I experienced a tremendous sense of worry. But I couldn't tell anyone about this. For a start, I didn't know what was happening to me and I certainly didn't want to pass these worries on to Wendy. All I could do was put on a calm appearance and carry on. And it wasn't as if I was given a chance to dwell on my feelings; they were just always there, in that creaking dam, the cracks growing wider as the bodies came thick and fast.

We parted company at the bottom of the stairwell and, as the woman walked off, we ran into the detective constable who'd been sick upon our arrival.

'You okay?' I enquired. 'Nasty job, that one.'

He was pale-faced but had recovered enough to speak. 'I wouldn't wish that death on anyone,' he said. 'But if you saw the victims of robberies and muggings here, as I have, every day, and if you'd seen what that does to a person's confidence. Transforms them, it does. Well, I don't appreciate the means, but I'm glad there's one less dealer living here today.'

As to whether DCS Melvin ever got his man, it was one of those cases where I never knew the outcome, simply because we weren't always told. Sometimes we'd find out because a trial was taking place and one of the profs would be called as a witness, or we'd see the detective and ask him: 'What happened to old so-and-so?' Otherwise we were often none the wiser.

PROFESSOR MANT AND I were called back to the same Peckham estate two days later. Another, somewhat odd symptom of estate life was the fact that, thanks to the close proximity of neighbours and how everyone lived on top of one another, it was (at least in those days) impossible to keep a crime scene from being overlooked and, in some cases, overrun.

When we arrived, it looked as though a festival was underway. People were hanging out of their windows in the five-storey U-shaped block. The reason for this was the fact that a body was lying behind a low wall, about a metre high, that acted as a narrow barrier between the estate's ground floor flats and the courtyard. There were hardly any police present, just two constables and a detective, DI Pemery, but the fire brigade was there in full force, having just extinguished a fire in the victim's flat.

Pemery apologised for the lack of a cordon, explaining that they were in the middle of a crime wave and Southwark's officers were thinly spread across the borough. The two constables, perhaps sensing the futility of any attempt, barely made any effort to keep people from ogling, so the prof and I found ourselves closely observed by about 50 amateur detectives, all smoking and chatting close by as we studied the body.

The victim was a woman, who had been in her twenties, and was naked and badly burned. Patches of her skin were scorched black while elsewhere it had peeled away from her body. She was folded up awkwardly and it was hard to examine her in the narrow gap between the low wall and the block of flats. Professor Mant clutched his back as he bent down for a closer look.

'Go on, Quincy!' a voice yelled from above, referencing the then-popular American TV show about a pathologist-come-detective. 'Tell us whodunit then!'

Ignoring the laughter, Professor Mant continued with his examination while I sketched the scene and took measurements. As I turned to take in the surroundings, I spotted a little boy, about five or six years old, break off from a group of his friends and run towards us. He leapt over the wall, landing right next to me, laughing as he did so before quickly clambering back over and running off again.

His parents (at least I presumed that's who they were), hanging out of a window just above us, made a joke out of it, yelling at him, 'Oh stop it, Michael!' with smiles on their faces as he continued to repeat his effort over and over, while the two constables looked on with disinterest.

'Cause of death looks like asphyxia by strangulation,' Professor Mant said eventually, waving over DI Pemery, who up until this point had been inside the flat. Professor Mant indicated the red scarf around the woman's neck.

'The burns came first, I'd say. Judging by the size and shape, it looks like she was tortured with an iron.'

'I'm guessing that the killer wanted to destroy the evidence by setting fire to the flat,' Pemery answered. 'But how come her body's out here for everyone to see?'

'That I cannot tell you,' Professor Mant said. This remained a mystery, although the murderer, the woman's boyfriend who had a long history of violent crime, was soon captured trying to board a ferry to France.

AN EVEN GREATER mystery took place in Peckham a short time after this, again with Professor Mant. We arrived at a 1950s prefabricated bungalow-style home to find that a fire had taken place. Nothing unusual about that, but the sight waiting for us inside was something I'd never expected to see.

As the detective led us inside, he said: 'We'd like to know whether this might have been a murder, or an attempt to conceal a murder, but I think you'll have your work cut out.'

The fire was confined to an armchair in the middle of the lounge. The frame of the armchair was all that remained, while at its base were two femur bones and the charred remains of two feet in a pair of molten rubber-soled men's slippers. Stepping in for a closer look we could see a pile of greasy human ash and bone fragments contained within the seat frame.

Professor Mant and I shared a dumbfounded glance. Could this be a genuine case of spontaneous human combustion (SHC)?

This strange, arguably pseudo-phenomenon hypothesises that fire can originate in the human body; it was discussed in detail in an article in the *British Medical Journal* in 1938. The authors stated that a certain set of characteristics were common to spontaneous human combustion:

- 'the victims are chronic alcoholics;
- they are usually elderly females;
- the body has not burned spontaneously, but some lighted substance has come into contact with it;
- the hands and feet usually fall off;
- the fire has caused very little damage to combustible things in contact with the body;

- the combustion of the body has left a residue of greasy and fetid ashes, very offensive in odour.'*

A two-year research project looking at 30 historical cases of alleged SHC was carried out in 1984 by science investigator Joe Nickell and forensic analyst John F. Fischer. Published in the journal of the *International Association of Arson Investigators*, their research revealed that victims alleged to have spontaneously combusted had been close to a potential source of fire, such as a candle, lamp or fireplace. They found that witnesses sometimes played down the presence of these sources, so that they'd have a mysterious tale to tell, or simply because they wanted to believe in SHC.

I surveyed the scene and spotted full ashtrays in every room. Several bottles of cheap scotch were in the kitchen bin. Our potential case of SHC was a heavy drinker and smoker.

'He quite possibly had a cardiac event while smoking,' Professor Mant said, 'and died from that. The cigarette set his dressing gown on fire and the chair stuffing provided the flames with a steady supply of fuel.'

At this time, in the 1980s, about four out of every five fire deaths were caused by dropped cigarettes.

'I'm surprised that the flames didn't spread,' I thought out loud, fascinated by this once-in-a-lifetime scene. The charred remains of the devastated armchair sat in the middle of what was otherwise an unmarked lounge, save for the

* Thurston, Gavin, 'Spontaneous Human Combustion', *The British Medical Journal*, 1938; 1: 1340

smoke damage, which had darkened the walls and left a fine residue on every surface.

'I've read about this,' Professor Mant said, 'but never seen it.' As he talked I took out my camera and started to take pictures. 'It's called the "wick effect". As the body burns, the fat melts, and this is soaked up by materials such as chair stuffing, which then burn upwards slowly but steadily, causing more body fat to be liquefied and so on and so on, until you end up with this. You can get close to a camp fire without burning yourself. Well, it's the same here.'

The man lived alone and had placed his favourite armchair in the middle of the lounge facing the TV. Nothing else was close enough to burn. He didn't have a smoke alarm, and thanks to the fact that his prefab home was detached and sheltered by an overgrown front garden, his neighbours hadn't seen what must have been a strange glow emanating from within.

These factory-built prefab homes had been erected here in the late 1940s and were only ever supposed to be temporary. They were an emergency measure to deal with the housing shortage after the Second World War. Over 156,000 of these homes were provided to councils across the UK and were supposed to be demolished by the late 1950s. When plans were put in place in the 1960s to replace them with flats, residents banded together and successfully fought to keep them. Some were still going strong at the start of the 21st century and the last remaining prefab, that once shared a street with our human candle, was sold to a developer in 2015 for £950,000.

WE HAD ONLY just left the scene when Professor Mant, who had the rare luxury of a car phone, installed for official purposes, received a call. A sixteen-year-old boy had been stabbed to death in a McDonald's restaurant in Peckham Rye.

By the time we arrived it was the Friday afternoon rush hour and the busy shopping street was thronging with people. A large crowd had congregated at the cordon – so large in fact, that Professor Mant and I had to push and shove our way through before a detective spotted us and guided us to the scene.

Standing next to the boy's body, which was curled up in a large pool of his own blood on the restaurant's floor, was DI Jon Canning. He nodded as we entered. 'I'm starting to think I should make you two my permanent partners,' he said, taking out a cigarette.

The body looked tiny, like a child's.

'How old was he?' Professor Mant asked.

'Sixteen. He lived with his parents on the nearby Consort Estate.'

'Small for his age,' Professor Mant said, lowering himself to take a closer look, wincing as he did so.

'We have a bunch of witnesses, so I think it's pretty clear cut. He was cleaning up after a busy lunch when a man entered the restaurant and attacked him. At first his colleagues thought he was punching the boy in the back but when they started to see the blood they realised he had a knife.'

'Four stab wounds,' Professor Mant said, 'all to the back.'

'This being Peckham, the young man's workmates weren't afraid of a knife. They piled into the attacker, holding him until we arrived. By then, his victim was dead.'

'Looks like one knife thrust slipped between the shoulder blade and ribcage, penetrating the heart. I'll know for certain once we conduct the PM, but judging by the grouping of the wounds I'd say this was a case of murder rather than manslaughter.'

Even though experience taught us to never assume anything in murder, I think we all imagined that the murderer must have held a grudge against his victim, most likely over a girlfriend, drugs or money.

Once DI Canning was able to investigate the killer's background, however, he found the truth to be quite different. The killer, who was in his early twenties, was a former psychiatric patient who had spent four years in Broadmoor for attacking a woman with a can opener. (Broadmoor was where Kenneth Erskine had been sent directly after his trial.)

Even worse, it turned out that the young man had argued that he shouldn't be let out, and psychiatrists at the Maudsley Hospital in Camberwell, where he had been receiving treatment since his release, had agreed and recommended that he be returned to Broadmoor. The prison, however, thought the young man was better served in the community.

So, the killer had taken matters into his own hands. He left his home on a Peckham estate with the aim of killing someone so that he would have to be returned to Broadmoor. The reason he chose his victim – a quiet, polite and hardworking sixteen-year-old boy – was because he was small and wouldn't put up any resistance.

At this time, despite the housing shortage, Peckham's estates were facing an exodus of people. Conditions had degenerated to such an extent that anyone who could find a way out took it. The annual turnover of homes on the estates was about 20 to 25 per cent, with up to 70 per cent of residents wishing to transfer to a different area. As homes were vacated and squatters moved in (only adding to the estate's air of decay), and as homes became hard to let, many new residents came from the nearby Maudsley Hospital and other psychiatric institutions, as ex-long-term patients – part of the so-called 'care in the community' programme (in reality a money-saving exercise dreamed up by the government).

Sure enough, after being found guilty of manslaughter on grounds of diminished responsibility, the killer was remanded in custody for an indefinite period. He didn't achieve his desire of being returned to Broadmoor, however, because it was full, so he was sent elsewhere.

The boy's heartbroken father told a newspaper: 'If I had my way this man would be hanged ... In ten years' time if I go down to Peckham and see him walk the street, I will kill him. I might go to jail for that, but I know inside myself I would be happier knowing the person who took my son from us is dead.'

WHEN TRYING TO place the blame for the situation in these estates, many people pointed to the government, which was trying to save money by cutting vital services used to support the poor and vulnerable. Although the North Peckham Estate was regenerated (with mixed success) in the early 2000s, it was too late for many people, and perhaps most infamously, it was too late for ten-year-old Damilola Taylor. In November 2000, Damilola was attacked by muggers in a dark stairwell in the North Peckham Estate. He fell on some broken glass, severing an artery in his thigh. His attackers, not much older than their victim, left Damilola to bleed to death. It took six years and three trials to identify and convict them of manslaughter.

Today, this pattern of increasing violent crime and societal degeneration is repeating, thanks to the so-called policy of austerity, brought about to help the coalition and later the Conservative government pay off the debts of UK-based banks who mismanaged their customers' money to such an extraordinary extent that they almost went bust. The government chose to give the banks £850 billion and, instead of asking the banks to pay it back with interest, decided to save money by cutting public services: from mental health to education; from community projects to housing. This decision has cost many people their lives, leading to an even worse situation than the one I saw in Peckham in the 1980s.

For example, in 2019 the All-Party Parliamentary Group (APPG) on Knife Crime published the results of a study which showed that the four areas of the country worst-hit by youth spending cuts (up to 91 per cent) between 2014 and 2018 saw some of the biggest rises in knife crime.

As MP Sarah Jones, who chairs the APPG made up of MPs and peers, said: youth services cannot just be 'nice to have ... We cannot hope to turn around the knife crime epidemic if we don't invest in our young people. Every time I speak to young people they say the same thing: they need more positive activities, safe spaces to spend time with friends and programmes to help them grow and develop.'

During the period studied, West Midlands Police saw an 87 per cent increase in knife crime; the Metropolitan Police a 47 per cent rise; Cambridgeshire Police a 95 per cent increase; and Thames Valley Police a 99 per cent increase. There were 732 knife killings in total in the UK in 2018, up from 655 in 2017 – the highest since 2007. Money might have been saved by closing community centres and youth programmes, but it costs several times as much to put all these cases through the system, and to get people through the courts, into prison and then on to parole services.

This at the same time as drastic cuts have been made to policing. Of course, a proper analysis is beyond the scope of this book, but to see the trouble we're in now one only has to pick up a copy of *Southwark News*, as I did one day in July 2018, and read how seventeen-year-old Katrina Makunova was stabbed to death; about two stabbings that took place streets apart in one day in Peckham; and how local residents marched in Rotherhithe to 'reclaim' the area after a mother was stabbed during a knifepoint robbery while out walking with her children.

Looking back at my files, the very next case I attended in Peckham that year was that of a young man stabbed to death in the street as he left a Chinese takeaway restaurant. His teenage muggers hadn't wanted his money; they were after his food. He'd put up a fight and ended up bleeding to death on the pavement.

If there's one thing I've learned in my time as a mortuary superintendent, it's that as soon as the government cuts vital public services, the body count starts to rise.

18

Uncomfortably numb

January–July 1987

'I thought I'd seen it all,' DCS Graham Melvin said as we gathered around the body of a murdered pensioner. 'From the Stockwell Strangler to the IRA bombs to child murders. But this, this …' His voice trailed off.

'Nothing surprises me anymore,' Professor Mant said quietly, 'ever since the war.'

Of course Professor Mant *had* seen it all. I'd recently attended one of his lectures (in which he sometimes delighted medical students by displaying actual murder weapons) where he described his work exposing some of the Nazis' inhuman experiments. By exhuming remains and interviewing survivors and suspects, he'd proved that (among countless other unspeakably cruel experiments) the SS had fired bullets into children's legs and let the wounds become infected so they could examine the onset of gangrene, and try out new treatment methods.

There was, on the face of it, nothing particularly unusual about the body lying in front of us. A 73-year-old man by the name of Harry Jones, from Peckham, most likely killed by a single stab wound to the abdomen.

The exceptional part of this crime was the murderer, who was awaiting interview at Southwark police station.

He was ten years old.

The boy, apparently an experienced cat burglar, had gained access to Mr Jones' house in the small hours of the previous night by climbing up a drainpipe at the back and slipping in through an open window. This was when Harry's wife of 40 years, 68-year-old Bernice, had heard a noise. As she went to investigate, the boy ran downstairs where Mr Jones tried to stop him leaving. The boy pulled out a knife and stabbed Mr Jones in the abdomen. Mr Jones bled to death in the back of an ambulance on the way to Guy's Hospital, Bernice holding his hand. A PM was always necessary in such cases; it was possible that Mr Jones had had a heart attack and it was this that had killed him, as opposed to the stab wound, and a defence lawyer would make the case that he might have survived the stabbing, reducing a murder case to one of manslaughter.

Professor Mant confirmed, however, that the cause of death in this instance was haemorrhaging due to a stab wound in the transverse colon of the abdomen. The boy, being ten years old, had just crossed the threshold of criminal responsibility and, after he accepted his guilt, he was given an indefinite sentence in youth custody, the length of which would be decided by psychiatrists.

MY OWN MENTAL state had become increasingly precarious. It seemed that in an effort to cope, my brain had shut down my emotional centres and I stumbled through the days and weeks in an increasing state of numbness. Outwardly, I looked to be coping just fine: I came when called and stayed late to clean up. I made sure that all the paperwork was completed and I somehow found time to give lectures on mortuary procedures to hospital nurses as well as the emergency services.

Southwark was one of the most – if not the most – challenging boroughs in the UK in which to be mortuary superintendent but, despite the lack of staff, certainly the lack of *competent* staff, the mortuary was somehow holding it together, just about, and I made it look like I was enjoying myself in the process.

Since Professor Johnson's death, Professor Mant and I had become a regular double act. With his neatly clipped moustache sitting on his stiff upper lip, his can-do tone of voice – often speaking between puffs on one of his trademark cigars – and his inexhaustible knowledge, coupled with his love of the job (which he pursued despite the agony of his bad back), Professor Mant was real inspiration. I aimed to live up to his stellar standard. And I did love the job; it was the only thing I'd ever wanted to do and the only thing I'd really ever felt passionate about, but at this time, the passion was gone. Inside, I had become a weary robot, like Marvin the Paranoid Android in Douglas Adams' *The Hitchhiker's Guide to the Galaxy*, who proclaims: 'Life. Loathe it or ignore it. You can't like it.' I didn't know what was wrong with me. Well, there was *nothing* wrong with me. I had no addictions, no particular weaknesses, certainly no physical ailments, and I coped, so I thought, with the never-ending sight of human tragedy and trauma well enough. I could feel, however, that something was wrong, although I didn't dare acknowledge it at the time. It was as if I was falling endlessly, tumbling through the days, from one case to the next, like a barrel lost in the high seas, keeping on keeping on because that's all I knew, despite the exhaustion and my growing workload.

THE BODY OF a 72-year-old man by the name of John Eyres had been admitted to the mortuary as a natural death, but, as I studied the body prior to examination, I noticed an indent in the man's head. A fracture to the skull and therefore a potential murder case.

Dr Stephen Cordner was the duty pathologist that day, and we travelled together to the scene of the death, the Camberwell Workhouse, aka 'the Spike', a huge Victorian warehouse-type building established in the 1850s. Its original purpose was to take in entire families who found themselves unemployed and homeless.

At the time Dr Cordner and I visited the Spike, it provided a much needed refuge for London's homeless. No one knew how it got its nickname but some guessed that it came from the tool that was used to break rocks, which was how the Spike's inhabitants used to earn their keep.

The Spike was known throughout London as a place where you would always find a bed for the night. Up to a thousand men could sleep in the 32 dormitories that each held around 30 narrow beds. There was a wing for the long-staying guests, or 'residents', who could stay on site day and night as long as they performed a few chores. Another wing held 'casuals', who queued at the gates each afternoon for a shower, a hot meal and a bed for the night. Many were alcoholics, or suffered from mental illness, while others were physically handicapped, or had epilepsy or tuberculosis. To the men that came to stay at the Spike, the disease, dirt and odours were less important than the fact that they were left alone.

An imposing building filled with so many residents, it was an intimidating place to visit. The body of Mr Eyres, who was one of the Spike's regulars, had been found in the laundry room. Dr Cordner and I carefully examined the scene but found nothing that to our minds looked suspicious, but, as was my habit, I made a detailed sketch of everything we saw, from the position of pipes and basins, down to a single towel that was lying on the floor.

Sure enough, the PM revealed a skull fracture as the cause of Mr Eyres' death and, after the ever-cautious Dr Cordner sought a second opinion from Professor Mant, it was concluded that this was indeed a murder. By the time the police arrived on the scene to conduct a thorough investigation, the laundry room had been washed down and cleaned, removing all trace evidence. However, the police soon identified a suspect – 58-year-old John Kelly, who staff had seen entering the washroom with Mr Eyres. He denied everything and there was no evidence available to prove otherwise.

The detective leading the case, a DCI Collins, called the mortuary and, after we told him we'd been to and sketched the scene, he asked to see my drawing, which revealed to him that a towel had been lying on the floor of the washroom. Searching Kelly's bunk, the police recovered his towel and sent it to Lambeth's police laboratory, whereupon the police scientists found the towel contained traces of Mr Eyres' blood. Kelly denied that his towel had been in the washroom at the time of the murder, but when police showed him my sketch he suddenly confessed to Eyres' murder and two more besides, both committed at the Spike. However, he was only ever charged with the Eyres murder.

He soon regretted his confession. 'I loved the Spike,' he told detectives, 'I didn't ever want to leave. They just let you do whatever you want.'

Kelly was sentenced to life.

The Spike closed shortly after the Eyres murder, with its residents sent either to psychiatric hospitals or smaller hostels.

This case should have been a cause for celebration. Thanks to my sketch, a murderer – possibly a serial murderer – had been caught and put away for the rest of his life. However, that night, after a few rounds in the Dickens Inn followed by a curry at the Khyber Pass with a handful of detectives and Dr West, I staggered home in a stupor of numbness. Wendy, as ever, was understanding about the pressures and strains of my job and my need to vent now and then with a blowout with the boys, but my strange mood was affecting her too, as well as our son. While I remained too dazed to know what was wrong with me, Wendy worried for us all.

And still they came, the endless procession of London's dead. A 44-year-old woman, who for years had endured the kicks and punches of her violent partner, had in between beatings bought him a Christmas card, addressed to 'My Darling Husband'. It was the first thing I noticed when I attended the scene, lying next to her body. Her message of love to her murderer, soaked in her own blood.

A 37-year-old cross-dresser found fully clothed and face down in the bath in his flat on the North Peckham Estate. A stab wound behind the man's left ear looked to be the likely cause but the PM revealed strangulation. The motive turned out to be drug-related – two young men were after this eccentric drug dealer's profits. Six years apiece for manslaughter.

A 27-year-old Irish labourer, found beneath scaffolding and in a garden backing on to the site where he'd been carrying bricks. Had he fallen or was he pushed? The victim had been paid the previous night but his pockets were empty. He had, after drinking heavily, fallen into an argument over a woman with two workmates. As they left the pub, still rowing, and passed by the building site, the murderers picked up a piece of scaffolding and hit the victim across the head. The two men took the victim's pay to make it look like robbery. Both were sent down for life.

A 41-year-old man who'd tried it on with the wife of one his friends. When his friend (who, like the couple, was incredibly drunk), caught them in the throes of passion, he picked up the object closest to him, which happened to be a glass ornamental fish, and smashed it into his former friend's face. The victim leapt up and ran out of the house (so they thought) and the married couple made up. They found him the following morning, having bled to death in their bathroom. Ten years for manslaughter.

A homeless man in his thirties found among bushes in Kennington Park, beaten to death, his face a mass of congealed blood. No one was convicted of his murder and the man was never identified.

And then, on Valentine's Day, an extraordinary case took place in a rather ordinary looking terraced house in Peckham. Although the scene was busy, full as it was with constables, detectives and forensic officers, the air was thick with the silence of a 'bad one', the kind of atmosphere where even the police's exceptionally dark humour could not penetrate. Lying on their respective beds were the bodies of a mother and her two teenage daughters. The father was sitting in the lounge, half of his head splattered against the far wall. He had shot his family and arranged the bodies in sleeping positions, before turning the gun on himself.

By July 1987 I was both physically and mentally exhausted. I'd dealt with over 11,000 bodies, supervised the exhumation of 21,000 remains, assisted 400 suspicious deaths and was heading for a massive break down.

Lurch hadn't been in for a few days and I'd barely missed him; he was in fact more trouble to me when he was in the building. He had recently muddled up the identities of two bodies – a suicide and a stinker – and the family of the suicide, wishing to see their relative, had been mistakenly told that his body was in an advanced state of decomposition, only adding to their already considerable distress, before I was able to clear up the matter.

After a long, hot morning in the PM room, Mary and I took a moment to rest in the staff room, which was when the phone rang. The caller, who turned out to be a doctor, informed me that Lurch was under quarantine.

'Quarantine? For what?'

'Tuberculosis,' the voice said.

I was, for a moment, speechless, but thinking about Lurch's lack of skills in the hygiene department, professionally and personally, this made perfect sense. London's air is thick with bacteria, not least with the tubercle bacillus, a major cause of tuberculosis (TB), a bacterial infection spread through inhaling tiny droplets from the coughs or sneezes of an infected person, which ravages the lungs and, if left untreated, can lead to death.

Before the development of the drugs streptomycin and isoniazid in the 1950s, TB was a common risk associated with mortuary work because those who had died of TB or associated conditions were frequently dealt with: people who had lived and died in poverty, in overcrowded slums, prisons, hostels and halfway houses.

By the 1980s, most people had assumed that TB had been eradicated, but the bacteria were still in the air, as they are to this day. And today, even though cases have been on the decline since a sudden upsurge in the early 2000s, London has the unfortunate distinction of being the TB capital of Europe, with about 5,000 people diagnosed each year.

It is difficult to catch, and you need to spend many hours in close contact with a person with infectious TB to be at risk of infection. Although Lurch (allegedly) worked in the mortuary, I barely saw him, so assumed my or anyone else's risk of infection remained low. Nevertheless, head office quite rightly went into overdrive. Biologists placed culture plates in the mortuary, which were monitored over a period of weeks. They all came back negative, and I was congratulated on the department's cleanliness.

The 'upside' was that TB took six months to treat. This meant that Lurch was out of the picture and, even better, head office instructed me to recruit a trainee technician. Finally, Lurch was gone, temporarily at least, and to my great surprise and delight I hit the jackpot. Robert Thompson, a tall, dark-haired, bespectacled man in his late twenties, was both intelligent and efficient. Despite never having worked in a mortuary before, he was a natural. It came to me as no surprise when, many years later, I learned that Robert had become captain of his own ship at Hammersmith and Fulham Mortuary and had assisted at Princess Diana's PM. Such was the weight that Robert lifted from my shoulders, I hoped that perhaps, at long last, I would be able to remain at Southwark's helm until the end of my career.

Robert's first case turned out to be unexpectedly dramatic. He called me down from my office to view our latest arrival, a decomposed male vagrant. Mary and Robert had started to undress the man, who looked to have been in his fifties, but stopped once they'd began to remove his trousers.

He was pretty filthy so it took a moment for me to take in what it was that the old man had tied to his legs with string.

'Good God!' I exclaimed, my eyes saucering. 'Is that what I think it is?'

Robert and Mary nodded.

There were bundles of £50 notes tied to the man's legs. Thanking my lucky stars that times had changed (I would have wound up on the slab if I'd tried to prevent George from dividing the spoils), I immediately ordered a coroner's officer to join us as a witness. We carefully unwrapped the soiled notes. They were greasy with years of accumulated grime and stank to high heaven but, once wiped, they looked perfectly acceptable. Once every last note had been removed, we took a count. The total came to £15,000.

Although we had a secure safe, I decided to take no chances and phoned the Borough Treasurer, who, holding his nose, took custody of the money in a plastic bag and went straight to the Bank of England, who agreed to honour the notes' time-honoured guarantee, despite the smell. I suspect they were immediately cremated after they were 'deposited'.

The vagrant, meanwhile, had no family and so was given a pauper's funeral, at the council's expense.

MY HOPES OF a stable ship were brief and were quickly dashed on the rocks of doom that evening when Mary entered my office, already in floods of tears.

'It's Eric,' she wailed as I asked her to take a seat. 'He's on the run!'

'On the run? I thought he was in prison.'

'They let him out a few weeks back but he got involved with some robbers and now the police are after him.'

This came as no surprise, but then Mary revealed that she had, while her husband was inside, split up with her police detective boyfriend and formed a new relationship with a plumber by the name of Dave, by all accounts a decent fellow.

'His whole family are threatening to do us both in. I've been to social services and they've sorted me out with a flat in Islington, but I need to get out of my old place as soon as possible. Would you be able to help me move, tonight?'

'But what about Dave?'

'He's away on a plumbing job. He'll join us as soon as he can but he can't get off work otherwise they'll sack him. Please, I'm sorry to ask but I'm really desperate, truly I am.'

I sighed. I simply couldn't abandon Mary to her fate.

That night, as the sun set, we arrived at her home on the eleventh floor of a South London tower block to collect her belongings. Mary fumbled for her keys and opened the front door. The first thing that stuck me was the strong smell of paint and then, a moment later, I saw the horrible truth. Vandalism. Glossy red paint covered her furniture and carpets while the designer clothes saved from her modelling days had been ripped to shreds. Her husband's family, unable to exact revenge on Mary's physical person had done the next worst thing. Mary picked up a shoe and tried to wipe off some of the paint with the remains of a torn dress.

I looked around, feeling awkward. I was an interloper, seeing something far too private. I didn't know what to say or do. Seeing how fragile Mary's world had been, I suddenly felt anxious about my own, as though it could fall apart at any moment. I looked over the balcony towards the setting sun and had a terrible premonition that the end was coming for me. In what shape or form I knew not, but I felt like a marked man.

A possible form arrived seconds later with the screech of tyres as an orange Ford Capri skidded to a halt at an angle in the car park. Mary screamed.

'Eric's brothers! They'll kill us!'

Three burly-looking men ran across the car park towards the block; one guarded the stairs while the others took the lift. I grabbed Mary's hand, pulled her out of the door and ran with her up the stairs to the seventeenth floor. Not the best move, perhaps, but at that moment it was all I could think of. I started knocking on doors. No one answered. We were doomed. I stood in front of Mary and thought I'd have a go at explaining who I was and see if that slowed the attackers down, but then the thought occurred to me that they would simply assume that I was the new boyfriend and throw me off the balcony. I decided we should descend a flight of stairs and try knocking on the flats below, but before I could move, two of the ugliest, angriest-looking men I've ever seen in my life appeared before us. I swallowed, seeing images of my broken body lying on the very slab where I'd performed countless PMs of similarly unfortunate souls, Professor Mant cutting into me to check I hadn't had a heart attack before they'd beaten me to a pulp.

And then came the blessed sound of the Metropolitan Police's blues and twos. Never had I felt so relieved in all my life. The sound was like an electric shock to the two men who instantly turned tail and ran.

Mary's boyfriend had come straight from work, spotted the brothers' car and immediately dialled 999 from a callbox.

I mistakenly presumed that this was the end of the matter, but all three brothers ended up taking refuge in Mary's flat, creating a siege situation. We quickly descended, and from the relative safety of the car park we watched as two vans of riot squad officers arrived. Wearing helmets, carrying shields and batons, they quickly made their way up to the eleventh floor. I had to restrain myself from cheering them on. The police mistakenly assumed Eric, top of their most-wanted list, was in the flat, and were going all in.

We weren't out of danger just yet, however, for another car pulled up alongside us and an older man and woman jumped out. These were Mary's in-laws and, before anyone could intervene, the woman had swung her right fist in a wide arc and punched Mary in the face. Leaping to her defence, I immediately received a flurry of blows to my head before, with the help of two police officers, we pulled Mary into the safety of a police car and the in-laws were arrested.

Meanwhile, all hell was breaking loose in Mary's flat – shouts and screams followed by some howls as the police quickly got the better of the terrible trio. Before long, they were trussed up, bloodied and bruised in the back of a police van.

Mary and I gave statements and, after discussing the situation with the police inspector, he agreed to help with the move the following day, even arranging a roadblock so that no one could follow the van containing what was left of Mary's belongings. Thanks to this kind inspector, the move went ahead without a hitch.

THE NEXT MORNING, exhausted, I returned to the mortuary and took a seat at my desk. 'I don't think Mary will be in for a while,' I told Robert, after explaining the previous night's events. 'We're in for a busy few weeks, I'm afraid.'

To make matters worse, as the day wore on, Mary's husband started calling the mortuary at least once an hour, demanding to be put through to his wife and to know her new address. Each time I refused and each time I received some exceptionally vile verbal abuse followed by threats to my life. At the end of the week, Mary phoned. She was in hospital but not thanks to any violence from her husband or in-laws: she had caught tuberculosis!

The council immediately relaunched its contagious disease plan. Once again the mortuary passed all the biological tests, as did Robert, myself, the coroner's officers, the tea lady and anyone else who'd come into contact with Mary.

WITH MARY AND Lurch out of the picture, Robert and I battled to keep the service going. As Robert lived right at the top of North London, I was left with no choice but to place myself on permanent night-call. On top of this, further problems arose with the mortuary's mechanics. Just as another long, hot summer got underway, a seemingly impossible-to-diagnose electrical fault meant that the air conditioning and refrigeration units only worked sporadically, leaving us in an oven of rotting flesh.

Around this time, a friend who worked as a senior health inspector based at Southwark Council's HQ asked me a favour. His fiancée had applied to be a police photographer, and wanted to photograph a PM for her portfolio. Though unusual, I saw no problem, providing the identity of the body was not revealed in any image. The photography went ahead, and I thought no more of it.

A month later, with an overheated Robert and I at the end of our tether, I received yet another late-night phone call from Mary's husband.

'I've got a right to know where my wife is!' he demanded.

'You know what my answer is, Eric. I'm not going to tell you.'

'You fucking idiot, Everett! Don't you see how that evil little bitch has got you twisted around her little finger?'

I sighed. 'What are you going on about now?'

'She's been stealing from the mortuary for months. Think about it. The watches, the cash: things always went missing when she was on duty!'

I hung up and at first dismissed Eric's claims as the ravings of a jealous husband. Mary, although erratic in attendance and having provided more excitement than I could ever have wished for, was well-liked by everyone, generally did a good job and earned a high salary. But the thought kept returning to me and, after some consideration, I realised that Eric might just be right. As Sherlock Holmes had once said: 'Once you eliminate the impossible, whatever remains, no matter how improbable, must be the truth.'

I had been so oblivious, so wrapped up in my own world of overheated overwork, combined with a lack of support from the council, that I hadn't seen what was right under my nose. After a restless night, I called Mary and demanded to know whether she'd stolen anything from the mortuary. To my surprise, she made no attempt at denial and calmly and coldly admitted her guilt.

She'd been discharged from hospital and was out of quarantine, so I asked her to come to the office. This time, remembering how the council had been prepared to cover up George's guilt, allowing him to go on to ever greater criminal heights, I was going to go straight to the police.

Mary arrived just as Robert and I were completing the paperwork for that day's admissions. Her clothes were dishevelled and she seemed to have aged dramatically; her ashen face bore the weight of her many recent travails. Once we were in my office, she told me everything, confessing to several thefts.

'But the thing is, Mary,' I said in frustration, 'I don't understand why. When you were making a good salary and had no reason to steal, why did you do it?'

'I did it for Eric. I wanted to give him something nice when he got out of prison.'

'Eric put you up to it, didn't he? He found out about the previous thefts and thought this would make a nice sideline for him, that he'd make some easy money.'

Mary shrugged and stayed silent. Despite my urging, she refused to implicate Eric, so I suggested she hand herself in to the police. We walked to Southwark police station, and a short time later detectives from the CID searched Mary's home. They found nothing; Eric had long ago taken the stolen goods, including the Rolex watch, and fled. Mary was taken to a cell and I returned to the mortuary where I wrote a concise report, delivering it in person to the Director of Service who demanded to know why I hadn't come to him first. He would have dealt with it in-house; now there was danger of a scandal. 'Because you would have done nothing,' I said, before quickly taking my leave.

A few days later, early in the morning, Robert appeared at the door to my office. His worried expression told me that something was very wrong.

'What is it?' I asked.

'A funeral director's just told me that he's been told that all future deaths are going to be taken to Westminster Mortuary. He wants to know why.'

'Him and me both,' I said, before opening a confidential memo that told me to report to head office the following morning, with union representation.

Early the next day I travelled to the council's HQ and was shown in to an interview room where a woman in her early thirties was already seated. She was slight, pale and informed me in a quavering voice that she was my union rep. She sat in nervous silence throughout the whole meeting and was about as useful as a chocolate teapot.

A few minutes later, Southwark's Senior Administrative Officer and the Director of Personnel joined us. They seemed more nervous than I was and talked for a while about the mortuary and its problems but didn't accuse me of anything. They mentioned the PM photographs taken by my friend's fiancée as something that was unauthorised and perhaps unethical, but only in passing. Finally, I decided I'd had enough and spoke up about the fact that corruption was inevitable when a public body receives no support from the council, adding that I had received no support since the day I arrived. After I was done, they told me to wait and went to speak with the Director and Deputy Director of Service. My union rep chose this moment to reveal that she'd been told that the council wanted to close the mortuary. I took this with a pinch of salt; the Director had threatened closure on several occasions, either because of the dilapidated building, the failed renovations, the thefts, staff absences, or a combination of all of the above. But the truth of the matter was that Southwark could not manage without a mortuary.

After half an hour, I started to feel like the guilty prisoner awaiting the judge's verdict. Eventually, the two men returned. I was to be suspended on full pay pending a full inquiry.

'Suspended?' I asked, incredulous. 'But why? I've done nothing wrong.'

'It would not be proper for us to comment at this time,' the Director of Personnel replied. 'Hand over your pass. My colleague will accompany you to the mortuary to collect the keys. The mortuary will close, for now at least.'

I went into a state of shock. I had been in denial until the moment it happened. If I had known it was coming, I would have emptied the building of my personal belongings, including my files and diaries. As it turned out, I never got the chance to collect anything (including my Omega watch, Mont Blanc fountain pen, several pipes and boxes of personal papers and rare books I kept at the mortuary thanks to a lack of space at home). None of these items were ever returned to me.

The Senior Admin Officer drove me back to my apartment above the mortuary to collect my keys and security passes. The realisation suddenly hit me that I would never enter a mortuary again until I was in the horizontal position. I stood, dumbfounded by this thought, in the hallway of my home as the reality of my situation sunk in. The council's senior management were closing ranks. I was going to be blamed as the source for everything that had gone wrong at the mortuary since I had arrived.

My son, who was now five years old, was playing happily with his toys in the living room while Wendy was cooking the evening meal, singing a cheerful song. The scene was one of domestic bliss but all I felt was a sensation of doom and despair; I couldn't go on. The stress that had been building up inside of me for the past few years came out in a terrible, blood-curling scream.

19

Losing it

July 1987

I continued to wail as Wendy telephoned our local GP who, realising I was in the middle of a breakdown and was most likely, in my current state of mind, a risk to myself, came straight over.

'Peter,' he said, speaking loudly and clearly, trying to penetrate my sobs, 'will you let me take you to Guy's casualty department?'

He escorted me, leading me along on the short walk to Guy's as if I were a lost child. A psychiatrist took me to a side room where, between bouts of extended weeping, and with a huge effort, I managed to respond to some of his questions. I was classed as being 'a danger to self' and was admitted to the psychiatric unit as a voluntary patient.

I was in fact half-conscious of my state, as if a small part of me was watching helplessly from the wings as I fell apart, and I was genuinely terrified of what I might do if left to my own devices – especially if I was forced to return home, to the mortuary building. After all I had seen all too often the results of mental breakdown, and not just the suicides but the actions of men who had snapped because of intolerable stress: the father who shot his wife and two daughters on Valentine's Day, for example. Or the man who had punched his wife in the face, killing her, going into denial, keeping her body for four days, washing and dressing her each morning until she turned green. Then there was the man who came home from work after losing his job and hit his wife on the head with a poker, killing her. The man cut his wrists but, failing to bleed to death, tried to hang himself. The rope broke, so in final desperation he stabbed himself in the heart.

It wasn't that I would ever consider hurting my family, or myself for that matter, but right then I had genuinely lost control of my mind. Something had broken and I could make little sense of anything and I was scared. My mind was rudderless, tossing in hurricane seas, torrential and unconnected thoughts raining down upon me in no apparent order. At least while in the psychiatric unit I could leave every aspect of my life to the doctors and nurses and not worry about the outside world.

Wendy happened to be a sister on Guy's maternity ward at this time. Every morning, on her way to work, she would wave at my eleventh floor window. I would see her, but failed to acknowledge her wave. Not because I didn't want to; I just wasn't 'present'; everything seemed so distant, as if I were viewing the world through the wrong end of a pair of binoculars. The one thing I did respond to was the mortuary rooftop, visible in the distance, which, when I first recognised it, sent me into a state of panic. The psychiatrist explained that the purpose of placing me in a ward was to keep me away from my home, which also happened to be the mortuary, the source of my trauma, and this small incident proved him quite right.

Wendy had been more of a rock than I had ever realised; she had been patient with me, remained calm when I was eye-deep in an undercover operation. She had let me race off at all hours of the day and night, during weekends and holidays, missing family events because the examination of yet another dead body couldn't wait. As a midwife, she had more than enough drama to deal with at her own work as it was. Slowly, as my time away from the mortuary increased, I started to realise the strain I must have placed her under, not to mention my young son, who was just starting school. I had missed too much of his childhood and now I hated the thought that I might become this death-obsessed, doom-laden stranger to him. In fact, as Wendy would later tell me, I'd already scared him during his first visit to the hospital by shuffling around the ward like a zombie, wide-eyed and vacant. I couldn't even follow Wendy's attempts to get me talking; I couldn't hold the threads together. She wisely decided not to bring him with her to the hospital anymore, lest my condition warp his mind so much that he would remain in fear of me for the rest of his life.

The doctors kept telling me that I would get better, but the merest thought of leaving threw me into a panic and I would have to retreat to my bed, stare at the wall and try to empty my mind of thought. This proved impossible; thoughts of my life and the mortuary roiled around inside my head like paper boats in a gale force storm. I wanted to explain what I was going through, but it was so hard to tell someone who's never been there what it was like to have lost control of your mind and yet still have some rational part of you able to watch in agonised frustration.

The doctors just let me be. They gave me no medicine and no therapy, only time. All I could do was batten down the hatches and hold on, hoping that this was the right course of action.

As the first week passed, I settled into a routine of staring out of the window or, when that became too much, staring at the wall, pausing only to eat my meals. As the second week got underway, emotions started to return: guilt and shame at having failed in my job – the very essence of who I was – at having failed my family and at my weakness for breaking down. Not so long ago, I'd been able to cope with anything and had delighted in the crazy workload, the responsibility and the challenge each day threw at me. Now, I couldn't even imagine going on a trip to the supermarket.

Coupled with this was rage directed at my employer, at the injustice, and I think it was this that got me moving again. Ten days into my stay, I picked up a pen, found some paper and started making detailed notes about my time at Southwark Mortuary, building a case against my suspension. As I finished each page, I pinned it to the wall by my bed until the wall was covered floor to ceiling. A doctor came and took notes but let everything be.

As I picked over the last six years or so, memories relevant to my current condition started flashing up. I'd occasionally heard stories from detectives about colleagues who'd had breakdowns, some of which had been fatal. There was the constable who walked into the Thames and drowned; a detective inspector who left a note on his door for his family, saying, 'I'm sorry. Don't come in. Call the police.' He'd hung himself in his living room. A chief inspector who had cut his wrists after his wife (whom he was divorcing) turned in a false report, accusing him of domestic violence. He survived but lost his job. At the time, I'd always dismissed these stories as being a case of people not being strong enough to handle the heat.

I also recalled that the police have a roll call of honour that immortalises those officers who have fallen in the line of duty. At this time, it struck me that there might be many more officers who'd fallen in the line of duty and whose names were not on that list – those who'd fallen while 'off duty'.

We'd all made the mistake of thinking we were invincible, that we could cope with anything when, of course, no one can.

It was only years later, decades in fact, that I realised I was most likely suffering from post-traumatic stress disorder (PTSD), a disorder caused by distressing events that leads to persistent mental and emotional stress, including experiencing depression and anxiety along with feelings of isolation, irritability and guilt, as well as physical symptoms such as headaches, dizziness, chest pains and stomach aches, all of which I'd suffered in recent months. One of the key symptoms of PTSD is finding oneself in a constant state of hyper-arousal, a kind of 'red alert' mode that the brain switches into at times of danger. It's both mentally and physically exhausting and destroys one's ability to concentrate, and this all too often leads to mental collapse and suicide.

Research in the UK into PTSD was pretty much non-existent at the time. The British Army, after decades of seeing sorrow as a weakness or nightmares as a sign of cowardice, has only in recent years acknowledged that it is a serious problem and now provides its officers with treatment. In 2010 more American soldiers – both enlisted men and women, and veterans – committed suicide than were killed in the wars in Iraq and Afghanistan. Twenty-four British soldiers died during the 1991 Gulf War, but the Ministry of Defence disclosed in 2010 that 169 veterans of the conflict had died from 'intentional self-harm' or in circumstances that led to open verdicts at inquests. Likewise, an estimated 264 Falklands veterans have committed suicide since the conflict ended, compared with 255 soldiers killed in action. It takes an average of fourteen years for veterans to ask for help with PTSD. Many suffer in silence – often harbouring suicidal thoughts – because they're reluctant to admit their vulnerability.

Of course, soldiers have a much more dangerous job than police officers, who in turn have a much more dangerous job than mortuary superintendents. But while most police officers may only see a dead body three or four times a year, and a murder victim even less than that, I had faced a never-ending torrent of the dead, from murdered babies and children, to people left horribly disfigured through accident or decomposition. While I was trained in the processes necessary to deal with dead bodies, I wasn't trained to process the aftermath. On top of this, I had been forced to face the stress of running a corrupt and understaffed mortuary with no support from my bosses.

I was never officially diagnosed with PTSD, but it remains my best guess. I certainly wasn't ever able to switch off and, in the run-up to the day of my breakdown, my normally robust pattern of exhausted sleep had been broken and I lay awake at night, case after case flying through my mind – PMs where I thought something might have been missed (Had that day's bodies all been correctly labelled, the property correctly stored, forms filled, fridges cleaned and samples sent to the lab?) – coupled with worries about what dramas Lurch and Mary might end up sending my way, Lurch thanks to his incompetence, Mary thanks to her dramatic personal life. Then, as the sky lightened, I had thought it was hardly worth going to sleep and that I'd better make an early start at the mortuary to check all of the above and see if anything urgent was on the way.

Although I had many regrets, I'd also had the pleasure of working with many brilliant minds – the many pathologists and detectives. But they would come and go, each part of their respective hospital and police departments. The mortuary was my kingdom, and I was both its ruler and janitor. I had fought to match the excellence of people like Professor Mant, in spite of the mortuary's shortcomings, with no support network to speak of.

But no excuse made it any easier to live with the fact that

mine had been a very public failure; the mortuary closure had made the news, with no real explanation from the council. Journalists – many of whom remembered the national corruption scandal that had originated at Southwark with George's trial a few years earlier – had already started sniffing around for an exclusive.

After two weeks at Guy's, I felt ready to go home and discharged myself. I was so grateful to have had this asylum, as strange as the experience had been. My state of mind was immediately tested when I heard the rumour that I'd been suspended for theft. At first, I dismissed this as typical mortuary gossip, but when it appeared in the *South London Press* I had to act. I sued the newspaper and they published an immediate apology and paid damages. Shortly after this *Private Eye* published a full page story about my suspension, blaming the closure on the council, asking: 'Now that Everett has been silenced, who else will dare come forward?'

Returning to our flat above the mortuary was a tough step but I held it together, and even managed to make my wary son giggle that first evening. I was determined to show him that his father was back and around for good now. A few days later, some friends asked if we'd like to join them for a break at their family's retreat, a cottage in Suffolk, for a couple of weeks and we gladly accepted.

Suffolk's wide-open skies proved to be the perfect place for me to continue to heal.

'When the vows said for better or worse,' I said to Wendy during one of our long walks in the country, 'I bet you didn't think it would get this bad.'

'I always knew you were a difficult proposition,' Wendy said with a smile. 'It's part of what attracted me to you.'

We found each other again that break, as wife and husband, and as mother and father. Long walks, lots of hot baths, lie-ins, light-hearted movies, family outings to the seaside and as little work-related chat as humanly possible. Not that I was repressing work, I was just starting to see that life could exist beyond the mortuary, that it could in fact be *better*. I was still exhausted and would sometimes find myself in a bit of a stupor, but my mood improved and my interest in life returned. For the first time for as long as I could remember, I rested, really and truly rested. Gradually, the turmoil in my mind subsided and, by the time we returned to London, I was ready to move on.

AFTER EIGHT WEEKS, with the council still not providing me with a reason for my suspension, my lawyer advised me to sue for constructive dismissal, but I had no desire to fight a court battle. I had enough savings to keep us going for a while, and the thought of a drawn-out court case was too much. Besides, my career was in tatters. My suspension, combined with the rumour-mill, made me unemployable in any mortuary (and most mortuary staff hadn't forgiven me for exposing the corruption which cost them a fortune in back taxes). I had no wish to return as superintendent of any mortuary.

My resignation was quickly accepted, and the council, relieved to see me go quietly, paid me three months' wages in lieu of notice and gave me a flat on a council estate in Dulwich.

A few weeks later, CID detectives captured Eric. Both he and Mary pleaded guilty to theft and were sentenced to nine months' imprisonment.

A friend at the council eventually told me the real reasons for my suspension. The first was that the council executives in charge were too scared to ask for yet more money to keep it going, to hire more staff and to make the necessary repairs to bring it up to standard. If they did so, then the council treasurer would want to know what had happened to the hundreds of thousands of pounds spent on all those renovations just a short time ago. By blaming me for poor management and for 'allowing' corruption to return, the council executives were off the hook and even saved themselves the cost of paying me a proper redundancy.

With financial support from my family, we enrolled my son at Alleyn's public school in Dulwich, but the local children, seeing a posh boy in his nice uniform on the estate, ambushed him on his way home one afternoon and beat him up. As Christmas arrived, our home was burgled and all of my son's Christmas presents were stolen. We soon abandoned the flat for a rented house in Dulwich Village.

I WAS AT this time regularly dreaming of the mortuary: not nightmares as such, but I'd spend the night dealing with imaginary murder cases. However, by now I was looking forward and, after a few more weeks' rest, I received an extraordinary and most unexpected phone call from Mike Morley, the producer of Carlton Television's *The Cook Report*.

He explained that Roger Cook was trying to expose the trade in human organs for his ITV show *The Cook Report*. 'Cookie', as he was known to his crew, was distinguished for creating a new kind of investigative journalism. He first exposed the underhand activities of criminals and con men, or failings in the judicial system and official incompetence, before confronting the protagonists with camera and microphone.

'You seem like just the man for the job,' Morley said.

'I'll have to think about it,' I replied. This was obviously something close to my heart, but was it also too close to my breakdown? Was this going to open up old wounds? Did I have the strength?

'I can tell you want to do it,' Wendy said, as I related the phone call to her that evening.

I smiled. 'I think I do.'

So, for the next three months I negotiated with doctors across the UK to 'buy' eyes, kidneys, hearts and brains. The take-up was frightening and embarrassingly simple to orchestrate. After making a few phone calls I found two professors who were willing to take brains off me, a Harley Street consultant wanting to buy eyes, and three technicians prepared to supply organs for a price (all of them were captured on tape).

I loved the work. Cookie had a large team of amazingly dedicated journalists who operated on an international scale exposing genuine horrors and miscarriages of justice. The climax of the show always came with Cookie's confrontations, when both reporter and film crew would be verbally and sometimes physically attacked as their target attempted to flee. Cookie has been described by the media as 'a cross between Meatloaf and the Equaliser', 'the bravest/most beaten-up journalist in Britain' and 'The Taped Crusader'. *The Cook Report* was watched by millions; at its peak it received 12 million viewers. It also won numerous awards including a British Academy of Film and Television Arts (BAFTA) award for '25 years of outstanding quality investigative reporting.'

I stayed with the team for a year, working on other programmes, including one about Satanic ritual abuse, and during a break between seasons, I was offered some freelance work as an investigative reporter for the national press. I soon found that I loved life on London's Fleet Street, where editors backed their journalists to the hilt and where there was a genuine sense of camaraderie. I could choose my hours and made time for my family. No longer did I smell of death, no longer did I go to bed wondering if I would receive a midnight call to murder.

Finally, I had discovered life.

Epilogue

The end that awaits us all

When I embarked on my journey into the world of death as a trainee mortuary assistant at University College Hospital, I needed to find a second job. The mortuary position was voluntary, and therefore unpaid, and so my savings soon ran low. One day, a funeral director arrived at the mortuary and announced that he had sacked an assistant for stealing a ring from a body. I stepped forward, offering myself to fill the vacant role, and the following Monday I started work as an assistant funeral director.

My new boss, Victor, was the director of a small firm based in North London, and his premises were like something out of a Charles Dickens novel. The basement, which acted as staff room/workshop/coffin storage, always had a fire going in the winter months. The company consisted of just three persons: Victor the director, a middle-aged, black-haired man who dressed impeccably in suit and tie on all occasions, save for the funerals for which he'd don the black funeral suit; Terry the driver, a pale-skinned man in his early thirties with an East End accent and a ready supply of roll-ups; and me.

We had one hearse. Pall-bearers and extra cars were hired in as needed. My first job was to visit a local carpenter's shop and collect two sacks of sawdust, which was used in the lining of the coffins. I had a long list of duties, and first and foremost among these was fitting out the coffins with 'inside sets'. This meant filling the base of the coffin with sawdust and stapling a silk sheet with a ruffled top to the sides before stuffing a silk pillowcase with yet more sawdust. Then, using wax, I'd polish the wood to a high shine before screwing the handles into place; brass for burials, plastic for cremations. Once this was done, I used a special machine to engrave the deceased's name and dates of birth and death onto a plaque (again, brass for burial, plastic for cremation). I enjoyed the work, preparing each coffin in the glow of the fire while Victor or Terry regaled me with stories about their adventures in the funeral business.

It wasn't long before I had my own stories to tell, suffering as I did the trials and tribulations of everyday life in a funeral firm. We were once on our way to a cremation in Golders Green when the hearse broke down. This not being the best time to call the AA, Victor and I had to get out and push. The hill was so steep and the cemetery so far away that we had to recruit the fitter members of the funeral party to pitch in. Victor gave them a discount.

On another occasion, we delivered a body to a funeral that was taking place at the Great Northern Cemetery (today it's known rather less grandly as New Southgate Cemetery). A thunderstorm was raging and torrential rain had turned the cemetery into a swamp. As we carried the body from the hearse to the grave, and the waiting mourners gathered under their umbrellas, Terry lost a shoe in the thick mud but limped on stoically. Once we got the coffin to the grave, we placed it on the two planks covering the hole, ready to lower it down, which was when one of the planks snapped and poor Victor disappeared with the coffin into the watery grave with a splash. By the time we pulled him out, he looked like the Swamp Thing.

Overall, however, my time as an assistant funeral director proved relatively uneventful, if educational. I was surprised when I learned that one of our main duties was the collection of dead bodies from people's homes, known as 'removals'. I'd assumed that someone else did that and we prepared the bodies and performed the funerals, but removals proved to be a core part of the service. We performed this duty about two or three times a day.

One day, we were called to collect an old lady who had died in her sleep in her council flat in Camden. Crowds were gathered outside; she was a popular lady and everyone wanted to pay their respects. Over and over again I heard people say how sorry they were that she had died; how lovely she'd been; how she'd never hesitated to help a friend in need; how she'd worked tirelessly for her community, helping old folk who'd fallen on hard times, always baking a cake for the church raffle and tending the community gardens. The deceased lady's face was a picture of serenity and happiness and I understood then that hers had been a life well-lived.

Our very next call was to Bishop's Avenue in Hampstead. Bishop's Avenue was known as 'Millionaire's Row' (today it's 'Billionaire's Row') with good reason. Homes sell for tens of millions of pounds and residents include sheikhs, princes and presidents. We had been summoned to a house which was the size and style of a Greco-Roman temple, and we followed a tall, sepulchral butler up a marble staircase to the master bedroom, passing works of art hanging on the wall, as well as statues, urns and mosaics.

The deceased had, like the little old lady, lived alone (save for his staff) and had died in bed. But his face was drawn, pinched with deep lines turned down at the mouth. Also present, apart from the butler, who gave me the impression that he couldn't wait to leave, were the man's son and daughter, both in their middle age. They resembled their father, both having the same downturned mouths. They were discussing their father's estate; in particular how soon they could meet their solicitor to make the necessary arrangements for the reading of the will. We took the frail body downstairs and placed it into the back of the hearse, which was when Victor realised that he'd left his wallet on the bedside table. He'd taken it out to present the man's son and daughter with his card. I dashed upstairs to retrieve it but, upon hearing voices coming from the bedroom, I hesitated. As I raised my hand to knock, I heard the son utter the phrase: 'miserly old bastard', suggesting to me that while the man had obviously done well materially speaking, his life had perhaps not been as rich as the little old lady's.

In this line of work, one can't help but wonder about why people choose to spend their time on earth engaged in certain pursuits, particularly in the pursuit of money. This thought would strike me most often while I was in the mortuary, perhaps refrigerating the body of an 85-year-old former road sweeper next to a 45-year-old stockbroker, both having died of heart attacks. Rich or poor, the same end awaits us all; everyone shares the same mortuary refrigerator. Similarly, at the crematorium (our local was Golders Green which was, ironically, owned by a tobacco company), rich and poor alike went up in smoke.

While working with Victor and Terry, I noticed that the 'happiest' funerals were often hosted by the poorest families. It was wonderful to see relatives really wanting to give their loved ones the best possible send-off, to the extent that they would themselves suffer financial hardship as a result. These were genuine celebrations of life, and, even though we could see the family, friends and neighbours had already broken the bank to give the deceased the best possible funeral, a £5 note would without fail be pushed into my hand, to give the funeral team a thank-you drink.

Wealthy funerals could be spectacular, with a dozen cars and a hearse carrying flowers while the coffin was borne on a glass carriage, drawn by four black horses, but these were invariably dull affairs where people seemed to have come for the sake of appearance and seemed to me to be going through the motions. No one wealthy ever tipped.

Now, I don't mean to say that the pursuit of money is the root of all misery, but I do know from bitter experience that some ways of spending your highly limited time here on earth are better than others. All too often, the pursuit of money or power or a career sends us headlong into a strange maelstrom of our own making. Trust me, life can be over before you know it. It pays to stop and take a good look around every once in a while, to see where you're headed. Because of the stress I was under while at Southwark, I was bound for an early grave. Luckily for me, I managed to transform life from something I dreaded into something I loved.

As to what's 'better' exactly, I'm afraid I can't be of much help. It's hard to imagine anyone who lived a more productive and enjoyable life than Professor Keith Mant. He died of natural causes at his home in Walton on Thames on 11 October 2000, aged 81. The prof loved people (dead or alive), and every year he invited students to spend Christmas with him at his family home where he made a great scene of expertly dissecting the turkey, much to the horror of his beloved wife Heather. He met Heather in occupied Germany, where she was teaching in a British Forces school. They had three children and were married for 42 years before she died in 1989. After the prof retired, shortly before my breakdown, he continued to lecture and occasionally accepted independent commissions as a pathologist. But he also got to spend lots more time with his orchids (he won prizes at flower shows) as well as trout fishing.

Similarly, Dr Iain West also packed a great deal into his life, a life he lived with great energy and enthusiasm. He died much younger however, aged just 57 in 2001, by which time he was arguably Britain's leading forensic pathologist. He had also taken over Professor Mant's role as head of Guy's Forensic Pathology Unit. His achievements were many: he was president-elect of the British Association in Forensic Medicine, and an active member of the Home Office policy advisory board for forensic pathology. In my opinion, his full-speed do-it-all-now approach to life (overworking, drinking, smoking and partying late into the night) shortened his life (he died of lung cancer). He was survived by his wife (a fellow pathologist) and two children from two marriages. In the years before his death, he bought a manor house in Sussex, and with the same determination he brought to his career, he set about restoring its huge garden, while at the same time developing a fascination with rifles and a love of wild-boar hunting.

Two extraordinary lives, lived to the full by very different characters with significantly different lifespans. But who could say in this instance that one life was lived better than another? If Dr West had not worked and played so hard, he might have lived longer, but then he would have been a different person and perhaps less happy as a result. He certainly managed to cram a lot into just 57 years.

But then there was Professor Hugh Johnson, who died inside the Old Bailey from a massive heart attack, at the same age as Dr West, just 57 years old. He had lived his life, at least from my perspective, in a near constant state of furious alertness. His life was full of remarkable achievements and he was undoubtedly one of the nation's greatest pathologists, but I didn't ever get the impression that he was actually enjoying the experience very much. He had never really got over losing the Chair of Forensic Medicine at the London Hospital to Taffy Cameron and, when I look back at my memories of him, he always seemed to be angry or frustrated. While the PM might have found that Professor Johnson died of a sudden heart attack due to coronary atherosclerosis, I would suggest that the real cause was the stress he put himself under.

When I come to consider my own odd little life, I ask myself, knowing what I know now, what could I have done differently? What, if I could, would I change? The obvious answer is that I should have resigned from Southwark much sooner than I did, but that's easy to say with hindsight. When you're in that moment, caught up in all the confusion, the stress and anxiety, it's hard to see clearly beyond your immediate situation and to recognise that, no matter how bad things seem right now, you can change your situation. In no time at all, whatever's causing you seemingly unbearable stress will seem like ancient history.

Like Professor Mant, Professor Johnson and Dr West, I loved pathology. I loved working with the dead and I would choose to do it all again – going about it a little differently this time of course. Even so, as strange as it might seem, I'm grateful for my breakdown because it taught me to stop, look around and assess my life's trajectory. And that's the best advice I can give you – to take a moment to really look at where you're headed. A good way of doing this is to try writing your own obituary. Write about your life up to the present day and then continue describing what you would like to happen from now until the day you pass through the mortuary doors.

My breakdown has also taught me to recognise when exhaustion is drawing near. When it does, I think back to my time recovering in Suffolk, walking with Wendy and my son under those huge and peaceful skies. Then I remember what's most important to me, and I step back from the precipice. This approach, as simple as it seems, has brought me 32 years of happiness (so far).

AND FINALLY, LEST my gruesome tales of mortuary life have disturbed you, please rest easy. Your body is today in good hands. The UK's mortuaries are now housed in modern, well-lit and temperature-controlled buildings, with proper operating theatres and with qualified and vetted staff dressed in full protective clothing. Thefts and mix-ups are extremely rare. In 2017 I was commissioned by Al Jazeera TV to find out whether UK human organ harvesting still existed. Despite my best efforts, I'm delighted to report that I could find no corruption whatsoever. The dead finally rest in peace.

Dulwich Village
2019

Acknowledgements

All authors rely on the support of family and friends, and I am no exception. This work has taken eight years from concept to publication, and it could not have been published without the help and encouragement of the following people. First and foremost, I thank my amazing collaborator and co-writer, Kris Hollington, who worked tirelessly to get my story ready for publication. My agent Andrew Lownie and Icon's commissioning editor Kiera Jamison deserve my undying appreciation for their belief in and commitment to the project, along with editor Ellen Conlon, associate publisher Andrew Furlow, publicist Ruth Killick and marketing manager Lucy Cooper. I hope my constant bombardment of emails and phone calls didn't cause too much stress!

Last, but not least, I must thank four special friends who constantly pushed me to the keyboard and who read and reread early drafts: Tayla Goodman and Erin Carmichael who kept me sane throughout the project; John Bowler and George Walker who introduced me to the author's secret source of inspiration – fine wine at the Savile. Thank you all, and here's hoping, with the Grim Reaper's permission, I may return with a sequel!